HANNIBAL'S FOOTSTEPS

HANNIBAL'S FOOTSTEPS

Bernard Levin

JONATHAN CAPE
THIRTY-TWO BEDFORD SQUARE
LONDON

First published 1985
Copyright © 1985 by Bernard Levin

Jonathan Cape Ltd, 32 Bedford Square, London WC1B 3EL

British Library Cataloguing in Publication Data

Levin, Bernard
Hannibal's footsteps.
1. France, Southern—Description and travel
I. Title
914.4   804838 DC607.3

ISBN 0–224–02273–3

Typeset by Ace Filmsetting Ltd, Frome
Text printed in Gt Britain by
St Edmundsbury Press, Bury St Edmunds, Suffolk
Colour printed in Gt Britain by
Chorley & Pickersgill Ltd, Leeds

To Jen

Contents

Illustrations

Illustrations

Acknowledgments

My WARMEST THANKS are due to all those who facilitated my progress through France; I must single out M. Bernard of the Syndicat d'Initiative in Gap and Mrs Pauline Hallam of the French Tourist Office in London. I am very grateful for the hospitality of M. and Mme Jacques Mousset of the Château des Fines Roches, and that of the Mayor of St Apollinaire; the lavish generosity of M. Jacques Pic in Valence, and the patience and helpfulness of his entire *brigade*, matched the quality of his cuisine. The monks of Aiguebelle, and in particular Frère Paul, were also exceptionally helpful. Captain Mimi took care of me when I embarked upon his beloved Rhône, and M. Philippe Denuncques laboured unceasingly to keep me from harm on the Col des Aiguilles.

My assistant, Sally Chichester, was once again helpful far beyond anything that I was entitled to ask of her; in addition to her usual decipherment of my horrible handwriting, she had on this occasion to decipher my tape-recorded mumblings as well, and she typed the whole of the first, longest, draft of the book amid all her other duties, finishing it without complaint less than a week before Christmas.

Once again, also, I am grateful to Brian Inglis for his sharp-eyed reading of the proofs, and to Oula Jones of the Society of Indexers for her meticulous and imaginative undertaking of the highly-skilled work of compiling the Index. Betka Zamoyska was indefatigable and ingenious with research.

I thank also Michael Shaw and Sue Freathy of Curtis Brown, my agents, for their unfailing encouragement, and Tom Maschler, my publisher, for his own sympathetic understanding, as well as his assiduous and detailed editing.

The verse by A. E. Housman on p. 113 is reprinted by permission of Messrs Jonathan Cape.

The helpfulness of the team of six who made the series of television programmes accompanying this book was of a different order of magnitude altogether. I have therefore included, as an epilogue, a separate and most heartfelt tribute to them. But this is perhaps the most appropriate place to say that most of the stills photographs were taken by Graham Eggar, with others by Michael Hutchinson.

I wrote the book at Homewood Park, Freshford, the hotel–restaurant of Stephen and Penny Ross, where I spent much time trying to decide whether the warmth, comfort and thoughtfulness of the hotel were greater than the culinary splendours of the restaurant, or vice versa. I stayed a month, and at the end I had still not managed to answer the question; I look forward to many more visits, with or without a book to write, in which I may continue to wrestle happily with the problem, and meanwhile offer my unbounded thanks to Stephen and Penny and all their staff.

Camargue –
The Elephant Wakes

IT BEGAN INAUSPICIOUSLY. Orly-Sud is not the most romantic of places from which to take off in search of adventure, particularly at six o'clock in the morning, but that would have mattered less had it not been for the rumour, which speedily proved true, that the pilots of Air Inter had greeted the dawn by going on strike, so that it looked as though I would not be taking off at all. Joining the mob at the Information desk, I discovered that there was no Information to be had; my breakfast rendezvous in Aigues-Mortes was rapidly receding, and my adventure more rapidly still.

First, then, to telephone the news of my plight. I hurried off to the airport shop for some change, only to discover (not, alas, for the first time) why the French are not the most passionately loved of all the earth's peoples. Behind both cash registers sat ladies familiar with Gresham's Law and patriotically determined to prevent the collapse of the French economy through a run on the franc caused by importunate travellers seeking solid coin in place of insubstantial paper. Ah, non, we have no change; ah, oui, we know there is a strike; ah, non, we cannot think how then one may telephone. While the argument continued, a genuine customer approached, and as the till flew open, I saw in it at least a dozen paper-wrapped rolls of coins of every denomination, for change; the *tricoteuses* did not even blush.

The British, of course, are at their best in mutual adversity, presumably because they love adversity so much. For the Germans, the Austrians, the Dutch, the transaction would be effected without comment or surprise. The Italians would ask after your family while counting out the change, and the Americans would jostle one another for the privilege of *giving* you the coins. As for the Swiss, before the strike was ten minutes old they would have set up a bank of emergency telephones for stranded passengers. (The Swiss, though, wouldn't have had the strike in the first place.)

I solved the problem by buying seven newspapers, one by one, and proffering a banknote each time. As I finished telephoning, I heard shouts coming from the Information desk. A riot? A lynching? Things were definitely looking up, and I hurried off to join in the fun. There was none to be had; the excitement had been caused by the announcement that a plane would shortly be going to St Étienne. *But where is St Étienne?*

The day wore on; occasionally a blockade-runner left, for Quimper, Périgueux, Clermont-Ferrand. More and more unsuspecting travellers were arriving for flights that no longer existed, and Orly was beginning to silt up with the lost, until it looked like one of those scenes, familiar from television news programmes, of refugees fleeing from earthquakes or persecution.

See, see! A plane is going to Toulouse. That, surely, is in the south, is it not? Or am I thinking of Toulon? All I could remember of French geography was a riddle from my youth; why are a sailor's trousers like two French towns? Because they are Toulon and Toulouse; but that gave no clue to their whereabouts, besides being less funny now than I used to think it.

Back to the shop I went, to consult a map, quite prepared for the *tricoteuses* to tell me I couldn't look without buying. On to the ticket desk for an endorsement to Toulouse. 'But you were originally going to Nîmes', said the clerk. 'Yes', I replied. 'But, monsieur, Nîmes is far from Toulouse.' 'Yes, but it is even farther from Orly.' This dazzling display of logic convinced him, and soon I was airborne, then trainborne, finally taxiborne. It was a little late for breakfast, but I was in Aigues-Mortes, and the adventure could begin.

In a sense, it had begun when I was a boy, and by the oddest of routes. *The Fifth Form at St Dominic's*, by Talbot Baines Reed, is ghastly trash (not that I noticed at the age I was when I read it), and I doubt if it is widely read by schoolboys today; they demand rougher fare. I have forgotten everything about the book except the denouement, in which the hero, under a terrible cloud of suspicion (I think he had been accused – wrongly, of course – of cheating in an examination), manages to prove his innocence, while the real villain is unmasked. But the plot turns on a vital piece of paper that has been tucked into a copy of the *Satires* of Juvenal. I read *The Fifth Form at St Dominic's* before I went away to school, and thus before I had begun to study Latin; who Juvenal was, and for that matter what a Satire might be, I had no idea, but for a reason I am still unable to understand or even guess at, when I had finished the book and rejoiced in the triumph of virtue and the downfall of vice, there remained with me a curiosity as to the work on which the plot had hinged. Somehow, I got hold of a copy of Juvenal, presumably in the Loeb edition, and read it with bewilderment. But when I got to Satire X, *The Vanity of Human Wishes*, I discovered the existence of the great Carthaginian who was to become my hero:

> Weigh the dust of Hannibal; what do the mighty commander's ashes amount to now? Yet for him Africa was too small . . . He added Spain to his Empire, then he crossed the Pyrenees. Before him lay the Alps, drenched in snow . . . Italy lies prostrate; on he goes. 'It is nothing', he cries, 'until we are through the gates of Rome, until we pierce with the standards of Carthage the very heart of our foe.'

Juvenal was writing centuries after the death of Rome's most successful enemy, when the sun had already begun to set on the greatest Empire the world has ever seen. Yet he knew that Hannibal's name would still be as familiar to his readers as it was to their ancestors, and indeed as it still is to us. For Hannibal, two thousand years ago, captured the imagination of the world, and has never let it go.

Anyway, it was from Juvenal's twenty lines that I learned who Hannibal was and what he had done; in addition to the catalogue I have quoted, I also discovered (though this bit must have been quite incomprehensible to me) that he had split rocks with vinegar, and also that he had come to a bad end: he was defeated, he went into exile, he was obliged to humble himself before those who had given him refuge, he died by a ring (another detail that I could not have understood). Juvenal, as I learned some years later, was not a man whose spirits gladdened easily. But I like to think that even his cold heart would have warmed a little when he discovered that I had fulfilled his prophecy most expertly: 'Onward, you lunatic, over the frozen Alps, to become the delight of schoolboys . . . '

When I went to my boarding-school, I began to discover more about this dramatic figure who had captured my childish imagination. We did not, thank God, study Livy in my Latin class (Virgil was quite bad enough), and it was some time before I learned that ten books of his *Histories* were devoted to the second of the three struggles between Rome and Carthage, and contained the fullest account the world has of the life and achievements of Rome's great enemy. By the time I discovered *Salammbô*, therefore, I knew that Hamilcar Barca, the hero of Flaubert's novel (if that blood-soaked book can be said to have a hero), was Hannibal's father, and I knew also the story, almost too dramatic to be true, of the nine-year-old Hannibal's vow. When Hamilcar was appointed to the Carthaginian command in Spain, his son begged to be taken there, and was made to swear upon Carthage's holiest altar that he would always be an enemy to Rome. Only later did I learn that the man who grew up from that child would keep his vow, letter and spirit, as few vows in history had been kept. And I learned later also that when the child had sworn his man's oath, he embarked on a journey from which he was not to return for thirty-five years, and that in the course of his odyssey he would carry his native country's war into the heartlands of her enemy, and be recalled to Carthage just in time to fight, and lose, the battle that decided her fate.

As any schoolboy must be, I was thrilled by the elephants; to cross the Alps in winter was heroic enough (the most ancient legend in all this legend-filled story said that there had been no way through for man or beast until Hercules cut the passes), but to do it with thirty-seven elephants turned the story into magic. It was many years before there began to stir in me a desire to follow in Hannibal's footsteps, and of course my first thought was to do it on an elephant's back (an idea which I abandoned much more reluctantly and gradually than the obvious impracticability of it really demanded); when more modest thoughts replaced this grandiose one, I toyed with the idea of a camel, then a donkey, finally settling for my own two feet. Well, the army with which Hannibal had started out consisted of some 60,000 foot and 9000 horse, so I would be in good company.

We know tantalisingly little about the details of Hannibal's preparations for his march, apart from the account, a mixture of the most prosaic logistical thinking and, a haunting reminder of the Hobbesian bleakness that governed such times, of the problem of victualling so huge an army. Hannibal's Quartermaster-General, having done his calculations, declared that it was impossible unless the army could be inured to the practice of cannibalism. Hannibal considered the suggestion, but rejected it, probably not on grounds of squeamishness. At least, I thought, it was unlikely that the problem would affect me as starkly as it did Hannibal, any more than the Gaulish tribes, through whose territory I would also be passing, would be likely to attack me with anything worse than hotel bills. (Nor did I feel obliged, as he did, to take along a soothsayer to cast the omens, and if I had thought it necessary I trust I would have engaged a prophet with a less memorably inapposite name than his: Hannibal's holy man was called Bogus.)

With no really useful guidance from Hannibal's own list of stores, I began by taking down my old rucksack, which had served me so well on so many walking holidays in my youth. I was amazed and appalled by the weight of it; without so much as a handkerchief inside it, my collarbones began to creak ominously beneath its straps. Surely there was something lighter on the market?

I had reckoned without the passing years; delighted to discover that there had been a revolution in the design and manufacture of rucksacks (they had even changed their name, being known now as backpacks), I bought one that weighed as many ounces as my old one did pounds, yet so strong that the makers felt confident to offer the most remarkable guarantee I have ever heard of: given no matter how much ordinary use, they promised, they would replace it if it wore out at any point in the purchaser's lifetime.

First into my backpack went my Swiss army knife, the official, full-sized, schoolboy's dream – two penknives, three screwdrivers, a bottle-opener, a tin-opener, a corkscrew, a saw, scissors, a file, a fish-scaler, a ruler, a wire-stripper, a magnifying-glass, tweezers, a toothpick *and a thing for taking stones out of elephants' hooves*; I was equipped for any ordinary emergency, and a good few unlikely ones as well. From the old days, there remained my whistle (for summoning help), my all-enveloping cycle-cape (not for cycling but for walking in the rain), my rubber coat-hanger (it inflated into the top half of a torso, so that even a sweater could be dried on it and keep its shape), my compass (as a plaything only, since actually using it was precluded by my lack of any sense of direction) and my plastic mug (for drinking from mountain streams). To these I added some devices that, like the lightweight rucksack, did not exist in my day. The strangest was a collapsible plastic wash-basin weighing half an ounce (you pour water into it and as it fills the sides straighten, collapsing again when you pour the water out). In addition I had picked up a towel made of some strange plastic – bath-sheet size, it folded into a packet not much bigger than a matchbox – of which wonderful properties were promised; just dab yourself with it, the makers swore, and lo! you will be instantly dry, though you had just taken a shower beneath Niagara (I had only one occasion to test the claims made for it, which was just as well, because it had no effect at all, dab as I would). Even stranger (and, in the event, even less called upon) was a 'survival bag'; this was a huge transparent plastic sack, which also folded up into virtually nothing; trapped on a lonely mountainside with darkness and snow descending simultaneously, the lost traveller simply climbs into the sack and lives to sing its praises – especially if a St Bernard with a brandy-barrel round its neck should arrive in time.

Add to these a miniature quartz-driven alarm clock; drip-dry shirts; a sewing kit (any man educated at an English public school can sew); paper handkerchiefs; a pocket torch; a battery-operated razor, together with an unbreakable shaving mirror; reading matter (paperbacks only); and a pair of boots.

I thought first that I would rely on my ancient walking shoes, still going strong three decades after I had bought them; in the end, however, I decided that the terrain I would be traversing demanded something that came up above the ankle (a wise decision, as it turned out) and I set out to find a pair of comfortable boots.

The adjective very nearly proved my undoing; some of the things I put on my feet in the shops I visited would have had me confined to a wheelchair for the rest of my life if I had attempted to walk the plank in them, let alone cross the Alps. Yet I was assured wherever I went that if I ventured a single yard on to ground more rugged than a deep-pile carpet I would inevitably perish miserably unless my feet, ankles and calves were bound in leather so rigid that it could scarcely be dented with a pickaxe. I decided to risk the hideous fate I was promised, and bought – in a sale, moreover – a pair of handsome tan boots with uppers that were soft and flexible; the consequence was that throughout the journey they gave me not a moment's trouble. What is more, the enchanted boots gave me the opportunity for a boast that I dare swear few can match; because the laces that came with the boots were too short to tie firmly round the tops, I looked in at a bespoke shoemaker and asked if they had any bootlaces four feet long, whereupon Hans Sachs cut two such lengths from a large reel, fixed metal tags on to each end of both, and sold me the result for £1, thus making me the only man I have ever heard of with a pair of made-to-measure bootlaces. (With socks I was considerably less lucky; I wear only silk ones, which I deemed unsuitable for the task I was to set them, so I went to what I believe libel lawyers call 'a well-known Knightsbridge store' and bought six pairs of stout socks in pure wool. One pair wore into holes during the first day's walking, and none of the other five pairs survived as long as a week.)

Finally, I had to be practical in another respect altogether. To write and walk at the same time is impossible; to stop every hundred yards, whenever a thought occurs, to jot it down, very nearly so. I had to rely on modern technology in the shape of a mechanical notebook, a pocket recorder taking a tape no bigger than a packet of razor-blades. It dangled from my wrist, it could be animated with a flick of the thumb, and I could talk into it without slackening my stride. Like almost all journalists, I loathe the act of writing; with this machine I could sustain the illusion that I was working when I was only talking, and put off until I was safely home the job of making sense of my electronic notes. I was almost ready to go; all that remained was to put my straw hat upon my head and take my noble walking-stick in my hand.

The hat had been my companion for at least a quarter of a century. I bought it in Athens, to replace one that had flown from my head as I was eating a picnic lunch on the very edge of the cliff at Cape Sounion, where that magic temple stands, its blinding white marble set off by Homer's wine-dark sea rippling far below; the building is desecrated by the 'Byron' carved into one of the columns, though the implausible freshness of the incision suggests that someone rather later than the poet was risking the wrath of Poseidon. (Disconcerted by the loss of my hat at Sounion, I had consoled myself by remembering John Wesley's account of being beaten up by a mob of the scandalised orthodox. 'I lost my hat', he said, 'and never got it again, which cost me 1s. 6d., but so long as I was able I never ceased to preach the word of God to them'.) As for my stick, its knobby top worn shiny and comfortable by years under my hand, perhaps this trip might be the one on which the miracle, for which I had been waiting most of my life, would take place, and the dead branch would burst into blossom, to show that the sinner had found mercy in heaven. More practically, my stick, which like any good walking-stick should become an extension of the walker's arm, would serve me well on hills, provided I could remember, against all the dictates of instinct, the rule that when crossing a slope the stick should be held in the upper hand, not the lower.

Hannibal's troops, or most of them, marched all the way; I felt I could do no less. Besides, walking is itself a pleasure, and it is now a dying one; experts in evolutionary theory assure me that people will soon start to be born with brakes and accelerators already attached to their feet. But the fact that it is no longer *necessary* to walk everywhere, or indeed anywhere, does not mean it is *impossible*. I like walking; I like the steady rhythm that enables me to forget my feet and concentrate on sights, sounds and thoughts; I like the feeling of physical independence; I like to get tired naturally, rather than through the frustrations and irritations of city life, dominated by traffic and the telephone; I like the feel of my walking-stick and the firm pack held in place behind me; I like to see something in the distance – a green hill, a fine tree, a farmhouse, a church, a man plying a scythe – and approach slowly on foot rather than rush towards it on wheels.

And there was another reason – obvious, and perhaps childish, but none the less powerful for that – why I wanted to track Hannibal's route walking.

Much of Provence was Greek before it was Roman (Marseille, for instance), but it is the Romans whose traces the traveller sees in the walled cities of Aix, Arles, Nîmes, Orange, with their amphitheatres, their columns and their arches, their quarries (some still in use for their apparently inexhaustible limestone) and their aqueducts. The Pax Romana, of course, was in its infancy when the nine-year-old Hannibal swore his vow on the altar of Melquart, but even then it must have been clear to the farsighted in Rome as well as Carthage that the Mediterranean would sooner or later be dominated by one or the other, but never, peacefully, by both. There is a curiously modern ring to the accusations and counter-accusations, of broken treaties and forbidden incursions onto reserved 'spheres of influence', as well as to the accounts of embassies sent to negotiate fresh peace terms and returning with news of war. There is also a presage of Julius Caesar in Hannibal's fateful decision, taken when he captured Saguntum after an eight-month siege, to cross the River Ebro, the moment when *his* die was cast. Though Hannibal was first by a century and a half, it is the Rubicon, not the Ebro, that has survived in metaphor; Hannibal has had to be content with seeing his name turned into something like a swear-word–'O thou varlet! O thou wicked Hannibal', cries Elbow in *Measure for Measure* – and a threat – *Hannibal ad portas* – to make Roman children eat up their dinner, as nearly two millennia later English children were told that Boney would come and get them if they didn't behave.

What manner of man and leader was he? There can be no better answer than the one provided by Livy, whose history of Rome was more or less the official one, glorifying the Empire in its annals as Virgil did in its legends with the *Aeneid*. Livy had no reason to make a hero of his country's foe, but he could not refuse him the tribute his character had earned:

> The power to command and the willingness to obey seldom go together, but in Hannibal they went hand in hand. With reckless courage in facing dangers he combined the shrewdest judgment in dealing with them. There was nothing too arduous for his body or his spirit, nor was he affected by the greatest heat or the severest cold. He ate and drank not for enjoyment but only to sustain his strength. He woke and slept not according to the time of day or night but according to the demands of his work, and when he did finally go to his rest he needed neither silence round him nor softness beneath him; his troops became familiar with the sight of their commander lying on the bare earth among the guards and sentinels, wrapped only in his cloak ... On horse or on foot he was without compare as a fighting man; he was always the first to charge, the last to leave the battlefield.

One of the most interesting aspects of Livy's tribute is the need he felt to qualify it; but his criticisms of Hannibal's character, besides being supported by no evidence (indeed, there is evidence to suggest that the very opposite was true), smack immediately of propaganda, of the old trick of blackening the enemy's name since his valour cannot be questioned:

> ... his faults were as great as his virtues; he was inhumanly cruel, utterly perfidious, indifferent to truth and without any reverence for sanctity or even for the gods.

Hannibal remains a living presence. It is hardly surprising that he survives in the words of Virgil, Juvenal, Horace, Plutarch, Cicero and other Roman and Greek writers who lived within oral memory of his exploits, nor that he remains the subject of study by military historians and strategists for the series of pitched battles which for sixteen years he won against the Romans in Italy. And the argument over the disputed points of his route (where he crossed the Rhône, which valley he took eastward, which pass he used for the entry into Italy), though sterile, has continued for nearly two thousand years already – both Polybius and Livy, writing respectively some twenty years and one hundred and fifty years after Hannibal's death, are very snappish about those who cannot see that all the problems are now solved – and has thus further served to keep his name in print. Even so, there must be something more to explain the fascination Hannibal has exerted for so long. It worked upon Dante, who quotes Livy on that haunting image of the three bushels of gold rings collected from the Roman dead at Cannae; upon Petrarch, who quotes the fateful rebuke of Hannibal's cavalry commander, Maharbal, when his plan to make straight for Rome after Cannae was rejected by Hannibal – 'You know how to conquer, Hannibal, but not how to use your victory'; upon Montaigne, who describes the horror of the dying on the bloody field (as well as quoting Petrarch directly); upon poets, novelists, historians and biographers of every era and every land; and upon me. I believe that the clue to Hannibal's continuing hold on the imagination of millions who have never heard of Scipio (who did, after all, conquer him) is akin to the secret of the thrall in which Columbus must hold anyone who stops to contemplate the immensity of his voyage to the end of the world, or which grips those who read of the long trek west by the covered wagons that opened the continent of America, or above all which transfixes a reader of Xenophon's book. The march of the Ten Thousand made Xenophon immortal; Hannibal has lived on through eighty generations because of his stupendous feat in leading over the Alps a polyglot army, mostly of mercenaries, in winter, without roads or maps, fourteen centuries before the compass was invented.

Livy was much given to putting obviously invented speeches into the mouths of the leaders of both sides in the battles between Rome and Carthage; the finest of all these orations is the one given to Hannibal when his army faltered at the news that their route lay over the Alps. It is worth quoting at length (Livy puts it in *oratio obliqua*, but most translators have instinctively felt that it must be put in direct speech, and so do I):

I marvel at this terror that has suddenly entered breasts that have never quailed before. For so many years you have conquered; you did not leave Spain until all the people and all the land between the two seas lay under Carthaginian rule ... and you crossed the Ebro in anger, to expunge the very name of Rome and to liberate the world. Then, none of you thought the march too long, though it might stretch from the setting to the rising sun, yet now, when you can see that you have already completed the greater part of it, when you have

passed through the Pyrenees and their savage peoples, when you
have crossed the turbulent Rhône though thousands of Gauls sought
to bar your passage, when at last you have the Alps in view, and
know that on the other side lies Italy – why, at the very gates of the
enemy's home, you stop, exhausted. What do you think the Alps are,
other than high mountains? You may think them higher than the
Pyrenees, but no part of the earth touches the sky, nor is any part
unclimbable by man ... To take Saguntum, what dangers, what
labours, did you endure for eight months! Now it is Rome, the
world's greatest city, that you aim for: how can anything be so bitter
or laborious as to make you falter? Did not the Gauls once capture the
city that the Carthaginians now despair of even approaching? Then
either admit to having less spirit and courage than people you have
repeatedly vanquished in these last days, or take hope to finish your
journey in the field that lies between the Tiber and the walls of Rome.

Ebro or no Ebro, south of the Pyrenees Hannibal could plausibly claim
that Spain was Carthaginian-dominated territory. He had started from
what is now called Cartagena, but which to him was New Carthage,
founded expressly to mark the shift of Carthage's weight to Europe, as
her leaders began to realise that their own city would sooner or later be
attacked from the sea by the enemy that lay due north, across the
Tyrrhenian Sea. But once he was past the Pyrenees, it would be plain to
all that since he could have no interest in the territory of the Gauls, he
must be bound for Italy. The Second Punic War had begun, and before
it was over Rome was to be shaken to her foundations; she would never
be in such danger again until six hundred years later, when Alaric the
Visigoth stood triumphantly before the gates of the Imperial City.
    When Hannibal set out on his anabasis, his wife Imilce pleaded to be
allowed to accompany him and to share his ordeal and his hardships (or
so says Silius Italicus in his huge epic poem about Hannibal, *Punica*):

Have you forgotten that my life is nothing without you? Can you
refuse me the right to take part in your campaign? What is there in our
marriage, in our conjugal joys, that makes you believe that I, your
wife, would quail as we climbed the frozen mountains together? Do
not doubt a woman's fortitude; there is no danger that wifely love
will not face.

He refused her plea, and the long march began. Shortly before he crossed the Ebro, leaving behind the conquered Saguntum, he had his famous dream, one of the most vivid and symbol-filled ever recorded:

> A youth of godlike mien came to him and announced that Jove had sent him to lead Hannibal to Italy; he must follow, never letting his eyes stray from his guide. At first he felt fear, but stifled it and followed as he had been bidden, not glancing to either side, nor looking behind him. After a time, however, curiosity, which all men have, overcame him, and he longed to know what it was that lay behind him and that he had been forbidden to look upon. His eyes would no longer obey him, and he turned round. There he saw a huge serpent following him, and as it went trees and bushes were uprooted and fell, destroyed, while in the rear was a black cloud looming up with the noises of thunder. In the dream he asked what this terrible uproar might portend, and was told that he must face forward, asking no more questions, but accepting that the future must remain hidden.

The immediate future was clear enough. With his 60,000 infantry, 9000 cavalry and 37 elephants, he crossed or skirted the Pyrenees and made his way along the coast to the area where I now was, at Aigues-Mortes, on the edge of the Camargue. Aigues-Mortes means 'dead waters', and as I gazed around that strange moonscape land, which only in recent years has begun to come alive through the infinitely laborious process of washing the soil free of the salt with which it had been impregnated for centuries, I could understand how it got its name.

From the Constance Tower in the south-east corner, which was built by St Louis, and to the top of which there is a climb of 184 steps, Aigues-Mortes was an astonishing sight; looking down, I could see its perfectly rectangular shape, enclosed within remarkably well-preserved walls (though the moat has gone) studded with towers or gates in the corners and half-way along, and coloured by the red roofs of Provence; it looked exactly like a billiard-table, pockets and all. It was hard to realise, or at least to envisage, that the town once stood on the sea – indeed, Aigues-Mortes was built by St Louis as his starting-point for the Seventh and Eighth Crusades, though the ramparts date from the thirteenth century, built against the last wave of barbarian invasions. Since then, the silt has spread far beyond Aigues-Mortes, gradually hardening into solid land while the sea retired baffled in the face of this unexpected impertinence.

Descending the 184 steps, tottering with vertigo, I observed that the gates which pierce the walls, once so implacably guarded, now bristle only with signs directing the visitor to hotels, restaurants, cafés and the Boucherie Chevaline (etymologically a most unfortunate name for a butcher); my first stroll round the town brought a reminder of that curious French habit of naming streets after people (including not only writers but even politicians) and dates. The Italians have an occasional Street of March the Twenty-Second, and the British similarly commemorate a few figures from history, mostly the owners of the land on which the street was built, but for the French it is little short of mania. In this little town alone I noted the *rues* Émile Zola, Jean Jaurès, Gambetta, Victor Hugo, Rouget de L'Isle, Sadi Carnot, Pauline Rolland, Amiral Courbet (indeed, I stayed in the *rue* Amiral Courbet, and in the Hôtel St Louis, too), Anatole France, 4th September and of course 14th July. (There was also a *rue* Denfert-Rochereau; he has a Métro station in Paris to his name, too, but he surely deserves it, for it was he who during the Franco-Prussian war commanded the garrison of Belfort, which not only held out, uncaptured, until the end of the war, but refused to surrender even when France had capitulated, until Denfert-Rochereau was given a direct order by the French Government to open the gates.) Professor Richard Cobb, who knows more about France than most Frenchmen, has discovered in Paris a *rue* Dieu and an *impasse* Jésus, and even the most casual visitor to the capital must have noticed the mouth-filling Avenue of Peter the First of Serbia, to say nothing of the Avenue of the Elysian Fields, an example of *hubris* duly punished by the seedy, run-down, hamburger-strewn, billboard-defaced, souvenir-ridden mess which that once noble thoroughfare has become. (But who is an Englishman to talk, when his capital city contains the horror that Oxford Street is now?)

I have always wondered why the jumble of cafés in the central square of any little French town does not give rise to hopeless confusion on the part of both the waiters and the customers; how do those sitting outside, and those serving them, know which chairs and tables belong to which establishment? I don't know whether Aigues-Mortes is unique in its method, but the solution suddenly struck me as I was choosing a table for dinner. The restaurants were colour-coded; Le Minos, for instance, had dark green chairs and tablecloths, the Café du Glacier had red ones, L'Ostal d'Or had orange ones, and the façade of each restaurant was decorated in matching livery. It didn't work perfectly; during my meal I saw several customers trying to pay a waiter from another restaurant, and sometimes, I think, succeeding.

More exciting was the impromptu performance that accompanied my lamb with rosemary. The square, and the diners' peace, had been raucously disturbed by a busker with an ill-strummed guitar and an untuned voice; a live trademark, in the shape of a tame parrot, sat upon his shoulder. Whether the bird had finally tired of his performance, or whether it was suddenly overcome by wanderlust, was not clear, but it suddenly left its perch beside its master's ear and flew up into a handsome old plane tree that dominated the square. Putting down his instrument, the musician shinned up the tree, displaying considerable agility in doing so, as there was not a single branch less than twelve feet or so from the ground for him to cling to. The tree was in full leaf, and our hero disappeared into its bushiness. Once inside, however, it was clear that he could not see the parrot, which, being green, was camouflaged; as soon as the spectators realised this, they began to shout directions to him. But what with their different vantage points, and the fact that the parrot itself was on the move within the tree, the directions he was being given were contradictory, and, as they were all shouted at once ('à droite!' 'à gauche!' 'un peu plus haut!' 'beaucoup plus bas!'), largely unintelligible as well.

As it happened, the restaurant I had chosen was the one shaded by the tree, much of which hung directly over my table; as I heard the intrepid but invisible performer crashing and cursing in the leaves above me, I began to wonder whether he might soon land on my plate. Eventually, however, his head appeared from the interior of the tree, alarmingly high, and soon, as more of him became visible, it could be seen that the parrot, its impulsive flight regretted, was sitting calmly on his shoulder. The busker came down the tree as agilely as he had gone up it, leaped the last stretch to the ground, and landed amid tumultuous cheers from the whole square. In the collection that followed he must have made ten times what he could hope to gather from a week's music; and deserved it.

I left Aigues-Mortes very early the next morning; I paused to pass the time of day (seven o'clock, I recall) with the waiters who were already busy in the square, wiping the tables. They wished me a warm 'Bonne route', and crossing the road I wondered about the old French habit of throwing cobblestones at the police, or, failing the police, at one another. The street violence, first of the immediate post-war years and later of the *événements* of 1968, was frequently illustrated by pictures of cobbles flying through the air, but although at the time I studied the photographs with care, and scrutinised the accompanying reports no less thoroughly, I never managed to discover the answer to the question that has always puzzled me: how do you get a cobblestone out of the roadway in which it is embedded? No one could do it by hand, no spade would suffice, and a drill would have been too conspicuous, besides tending to smash the cobbles *in situ*. The cobbles have all been removed in Paris, and there are new missiles for more modern encounters with the law. But the mystery has never been cleared up: even the memoirs of reformed revolutionaries fail to deal with it. I put the thought aside – it was impossible to imagine a crowd in Aigues-Mortes resorting to any kind of violence, let alone tearing up the cobblestones – and passed through the gate that formed the middle pocket of the billiard-table.

The canals of the Camargue run straight, and there are hundreds of them, veining the map with blue, from the tiniest irrigation channels to the broad, river-like waterway, with its raised towpath, that I was following north-east to Gallician. The canals were clearly needed; I passed a hand-painted sign, as I left the road, reading 'Allez doucement, s'il vous plaît, on mange de la poussière', and so one did, for the ground was cracked like a chapped lip, and every step kicked up the dust. There were the usual fishermen, sitting contemplatively on the bank as fishermen have done ever since fish were invented: they were clearly catching nothing but obviously not minding. I think I could be a fisherman myself, and may well take up the sport in my old age (fancy having to fall back on bowls, or even golf!); the fish would feel safe, and I could wile away the hours most pleasantly, for it is a curious but surely significant fact that fishermen passed on a country walk always look happy. (I refer only to the fixed-line variety; those who are to be seen in the middle of a rushing river with waders up to their hips, dementedly throwing the line over the surface, are a different breed altogether, and presumably die early from the cold and wet.)

My direction-blindness obliged me to keep looking back, though since the canal had not yet produced a bend, let alone a tributary, even I could not have taken a wrong turning; in any case, the Constance Tower, with its lantern atop, remained in view, pointing to the heavens. Assuredly, those who built it for a lookout against approaching enemies did their work well, for in this flat country (and there was not so much as a bump or a hillock anywhere) the watchman could see for as many miles as his eyes could strain, and long before a hostile force approached the town the gates would have been shut. A little further along the canal, I encountered another mystery I shall never solve: the appeal of a houseboat. There were many parked along the canal, on both sides; whenever a moving boat passed, I noticed that the occupants looked significantly more cheerful than the glum residents, which only deepened the mystery; why be cabined, cribbed, confined, permanently damp *and* unhappy?

Infertile the Camargue may be, but the hardiness of nature is not to be denied. I have always marvelled at the way a wild flower or plant will find itself a berth on a bleak and inhospitable wall, or in the cracks of a pavement; if all else fails, the rootless kind will cling even to the smooth surface of a brick or stone. Along the canal, my boots were brushed by thickset clover and coarse grass sprinkled with poppies, and after a time man's ingenuity was matched to nature's; the vineyards that stretched to the horizon, and the bizarre outline of the umbrella pine, which always looks as though it must be topiary, marked the wresting back of the soil from the salt which had possessed it for so long. There were hundreds of butterflies, too; the sight of them made me realise that I had imperceptibly been hypnotised by the glittering eye of those who would persuade us that the gentlest and most delicately beautiful of all living things had been entirely wiped out by man and his poisonous chemicals. I distinguished the familiar tortoiseshell and cabbage-white, together with a tiny red one with black markings and an even smaller one in pale blue.

The Camargue, as even I knew before I set out on this, my first visit to it, is famous for its white horses, its black bulls and its pink flamingoes. I peered about, anxious for my first sighting of these celebrated creatures, and was rewarded first by a glimpse of the horses. I have read or heard somewhere that there is no such thing in nature as a truly white horse; it seems that they can get no further than a very pale grey. If so, the difference is not apparent to the eye, for the herd looked not just white, but dazzling marble, gleaming like the salt-pans beneath the brilliant sun. Their tails were long and bushy, and although they clearly had no fear of man – they eyed me incuriously and went on grazing – they were not like those degenerate creatures, the ponies of the New Forest, which will put their heads into a car to beg for sugar-lumps.

After the horses, the bulls, as black as the horses are white. I have always been terrified of bulls (and not much less so of cows), and the familiar fear returned at the sight of these; I approached them in a gingerly fashion, quite prepared to run for my life to avoid being trampled, gored or even eaten, but to my astonishment the whole herd trotted demurely away as I approached them. Could it really be that they were only so many Ferdinands, more afraid of me than I of them? The thought led me to another; are animals like these conscious of their own beauty? For beautiful they were; absolutely black, with no variation in shade anywhere on their sleek bodies, and all with the same sweeping curve of the horns. In among them waddled and fluttered countless white egrets, with the curious pelican-like bulge in the throat; one of them occasionally perched nonchalantly on a horn, and the contrast of the colours made me wish yet again that I could paint. Since this journey was partly designed to provide an opportunity for me to abandon the last of my vain regrets, such thoughts suggested that I was not exactly living up to the purpose so far.

An old farmhouse loomed up on the left of my path, perfectly proportioned, quite without selfconsciousness; it had plainly been built without an architect, but the harmony of its lines was beautiful, and the beauty was of that organic kind that comes from fitness-for-use. The shape and the materials must have been chosen because they seemed right to the builder and the future owner (if, indeed, these were not the same man), not because they conformed to any principle of design, even a good one. Where and when did Europe lose the instinct for making and building naturally? No doubt Blenheim needed an architect, but the little artisans' cottages of Georgian Bath were put up by builders who had never heard of the Golden Section, let alone pre-stressed concrete, and they are now sought after (those, that is, which the municipal authorities have so far failed to pull down) as though they were palaces themselves.

After lunch at Gallician I continued along the canal; now, however, there were occasional bushes and even trees, which gave welcome patches of shade as the heat of the day, undiminished by even the lightest breeze, burned down. The other side of the canal (this has been the story of my life) was thickly wooded, and I could see the matching path, cool and inviting; short of swimming across the canal, however, I had no means of getting to it, and could only admire the range of almost autumnal colours, from russet to olive-green, spread out so tantalisingly near.

St Gilles loomed up, preceded by a single monstrous factory chimney (with, as it proved, a monstrous factory beneath it). Just before I got to the outskirts, there was yet another mystery – a mystery to me, anyway: the game of *boules*. I have watched this idiotic pastime for what must by now be a formidable total of hours, and I have never been able to see any point to it at all; more, I have never been able to detect any sign that the players can see any point to it either. It is invariably played on a stretch of dust, and the metal balls are simply thrown back and forth without any discernible policy or pattern. The players never seem to keep any kind of score, nor have I ever seen any of them express satisfaction or disappointment with a throw. And yet the French seem to take it as seriously as the British do football; every village has its team and every café displays posters announcing the fortunes of the local league and the pennants that are presumably the trophies of victory. I stopped to watch the *boulistes* of St Gilles, in the hope that this time I might begin to understand the point at last. It was not to be.

Walking into the centre of St Gilles, I was suddenly hailed by a figure whom at first I took to be a retired pirate. He had a bushy beard, a flat cap and a rolling gait; he was among a bunch of his cronies, and I assumed that I had walked into the middle of one of those scenes of Provençal life with which Marcel Pagnol filled his Marseille trilogy. If so, my pirate was clearly playing the Raimu role, but to my astonishment he turned out to be an Englishman from Leeds, who had sailed his boat here three years ago, liked what he found, and decided to stay. He told me he had a little job at the local agricultural co-operative, that his pension arrived regularly, and that he went home only for Christmas.

Nevertheless, it *was* a scene from Pagnol. My pirate who had swallowed the anchor had his friends about him, and one of them could have fitted just as neatly as the pirate himself into the films, probably in the role of the thin, sad-looking one who is always being cuckolded. The St Gilles group held court at the tables outside a little café, and this member sat on a straight-backed wooden chair beside the door of it. He neither spoke nor moved for the three-quarters of an hour I stayed; he stared into the distance, without any expression on his face and without a drink. He might have been sitting there, in exactly the same way, since the 1930s; perhaps even when he died he would continue to sit upright on his upright chair and be pointed out to the passers-by. The Pagnolesque air made me long to stage one of the familiar scenes from the film, the one in which the allies put a bowler hat in the middle of the road, with a brick hidden under it; they calculate, correctly, that no one can see a bowler hat, apparently deserted, without kicking it, and one after another strangers approach, see the hat and take a swing at it, only to go howling and hopping away with a badly stubbed toe. But it was strange to think that this sleepy, gentle little town was the place where the Albigensian crusade began, to end in savagery hardly to be matched until our own century.

I spent the night in St Gilles; next morning I went to a Provençal ceremony stranger than even the game of *boules*, though considerably more exciting. This was the *férade*, the branding of the bulls, which is an excuse for a day-long outdoor party; I was cordially invited to join the village at the long lunch table stretched beside the field where the *férade* took place.

The ceremony was in two parts; one before lunch and one after; both, as far as I could see, marked an opportunity for the young bloods of the village to get first drunk and then drunker. A line of horsemen with long poles trotted up the field towards the bulls, accompanied, naturally, by the Toreador's Song from the mobile discotheque-van; the horsemen's object was to separate one bull from the herd and bring it back for the branding. When the bull, driven on before the mounted line, got near the business end of the field, the young bloods wrestled with the beast, one grabbing its tail, others leaping on to its back, even seizing its horns; beneath the combined assault the bull fell to the ground, whereupon all the bravos sat on it and the branding-iron was applied, to the accompaniment of a roar of fury and pain from the bull. Then the bravos all got off, and the real fun began. The bull got to its feet in a very bad temper; a desultory effort was made by the young men to head it in the direction of its fellows at the far end of the field, but a bull still smarting from a red-hot iron applied to its flank is unlikely to do as it is bidden, particularly if the bidding is at the behest of its tormentors; most of the marked bulls, therefore, charged straight at the crowd, which scattered in every direction, and occasionally in the same direction, forming a kind of mass conga-line round any fixed object, such as a tree-trunk, that seemed to offer an obstacle to the charging bull.

Lunch was merry, though I did not much fancy the chances of one or two of the young men who had been devotedly punishing the jugs of local wine and were planning to take part in the afternoon's sport of going into a makeshift arena with a bull and provoking it to charge; the winner was the one who remained until the bull was almost upon him before leaping the inner barrier to safety. The bull's horns were capped, I noticed, for this part of the ceremony, but although that meant that the bravos could not be gored, they could certainly be tossed, and in any case any of them leaving his escape a fraction of a second late would be liable to be struck by the weight of a bull transformed for the moment into a projectile. I asked about the danger, and received the perfect reply: It only happens once a year.

No one was hurt, and the hot afternoon wore sleepily on; eventually, the children were packed up (they had spent most of the day climbing on to the bull-pens, frequently levering themselves up by hanging on to the sign that said 'Défense de monter'), the disco-van fell silent, the tablecloths were folded away, and a scene that Dufy would not have scorned to paint came to an end.

I never saw any of the Camargue flamingoes.

1 First stop: boots off at Gallician   2 The canals of the Camargue run straight and walk long

3

2

Arles –
The Living Image

HANNIBAL CROSSED THE Rhône near Fourques, just outside Arles; his passage gave rise to one of the strangest and most picturesque of all the images of Hannibal's epic. Hostile Gauls had gathered on the eastern bank; he sent a detachment up-river to get across under cover of darkness, work their way down, station themselves behind the enemy and send up a smoke-signal when they were in position. The smoke was seen; the vanguard set off, the Gauls were attacked simultaneously from front and rear, and the day was easily won. But the sight that fixes the encounter for ever concerns the elephants; it is their first appearance on the stage, and they made a fittingly dramatic entry.

Huge fixed docks were built out from the western bank, and covered with earth to persuade the elephants that they were still on dry land; to the far end of these jetties smaller rafts had been attached. The unsuspecting animals (the females were led on first, nature thus ensuring that the males would follow) went confidently out into mid-stream, and as soon as they were all safely on the free-floating pontoons the ropes were cut, and the boats which had been waiting at the far end began to tow them across. Now surrounded by water, the elephants panicked, and some fell in. Many of the mahouts were drowned, but the elephants survived by literally snorkelling their way over; with only their trunks showing above the surface, they walked sedately across the Rhône, breathing through that strange elongated nose of theirs, which can rarely have been put to so extraordinary a use.

Or so says Polybius; we smile at the legend. Too soon; I made enquiry of zoological experts as to whether an elephant can survive under water by breathing through its trunk, and discovered that indeed it can.

Hannibal had his Hanno to prepare the success of the crossing; it was Hanno – or *a* Hanno – who commanded the detachment which ambushed the Gauls*. My Hanno was the redoubtable Captain Mimi, a weatherbeaten Popeye who had made himself an expert on every aspect of the Rhône – its history, its currents, its size and volume, its hydro-electricity, its fish, its birds, its traffic; for this occasion, I was its traffic. Hanno's detachment had been led by Hannibal's Spanish troops, who were all expert swimmers, but the first thing Hannibal did when he had finished pitching camp on the west bank was to buy up all the boats the cisrhodanean Gauls would sell him – an example of his political wisdom as well as his tactical shrewdness, for he had practised from the start a policy of conciliation and barter, rather than attack and seizure, with all the tribesmen who lay between him and his goal; his enemy was Rome, and he fought non-Romans only when they fought him first.

First, then, to hire a rowing-boat from Captain Mimi. He looked at me dubiously, clearly sceptical of my ability to row across his Rhône; little did he know that of all the forms of physical exercise known to man the only two I have ever practised with pleasure are walking and rowing, and the one I have practised not only for pleasure but with recognisable skill is the latter. He was finally convinced only when I expressed disappointment that the oars were fixed into the rowlocks by a metal bolt, so that they could not be feathered; my feathering has caused gasps of astonishment and admiration from onlookers on the bank for more than forty years. But the careful Captain, explaining that the Rhône's currents, though very much slower than they used to be before the hydro-electric works were built, could still be treacherous, followed me across in a motor-boat (which served also, of course, to tow the rowing-boat back).

With unfeathered oars I crossed the Rhône, aiming for a handsome stone lion perched on the farther bank; when I landed, I inspected him, and found that he was one of a pair, though the head of his brother lay, Ozymandias-like, beside the pedestal. I shook hands with Captain Mimi, and went my way.

---

*One of the problems with this story is the extraordinary paucity of names in Carthage; the student can distinguish (or more correctly cannot distinguish) seven Hamilcars, five Hasdrubals, two Himilcos and five Hannos.

Arles is Van Gogh's territory as well as Julius Caesar's (I was staying in the Hôtel Jules César). There is a Restaurant Van Gogh, and another which, deprived of his name, exhibits locally-painted copies of his work. But in the Place du Forum there is the café that he painted, instantly recognisable, and I took my seat outside it, opened a volume of his paintings, and struck the pose of his sitter, glass and all. I could see the statue in the centre of the square, which is not of Van Gogh, or even Caesar, but of Frédéric Mistral; closing the book, I faced the Frédéric Mistral problem, which lies in the obsession that Provence still has, or at any rate feels obliged to pretend it has, for him, his work and his achievement. The 'Félibrige', which he founded, was a movement designed to keep alive the Provençal language, a strange mixture of pidgin French, Spanish and what I take to be the original *langue d'oc*. His attempt to preserve Provençal (he even won the Nobel Prize for literature, presumably because none of the judges could understand a word of his writings) failed completely, even more completely than the similar attempts to persuade the Welsh to speak Welsh and the Irish to speak Gaelic; I doubt if more than one Frenchman in a thousand knows a word of it, and I amused myself by going into bookshops and asking (in vain) if they had a French–Provençal dictionary. (You can buy an Italian–Venetian dictionary in Venice, and you can even hear Venetian spoken there.) But what makes Mistral and his endeavours today more tiresome than even the Welsh Language Society is the fey nonsense with which he invested Provençal life; for him, it was not only the language, but a misty amalgam of culture, history and religion. Studying his statue more closely, I formulated a Theorem: in statuary and portraiture, the softness of the subject's hat and the floppiness of his cravat are in indirect proportion to the seriousness with which it is necessary to take him, so that a figure wearing an infinitely soft hat and infinitely floppy cravat makes it infinitely unnecessary to take him seriously at all. From then on, I greeted every *rue* Frédéric Mistral, *place* Frédéric Mistral, *bar* Frédéric Mistral and *boulangerie* Frédéric Mistral with thumb to nose.

Mistral's only defence, as far as I was concerned, consisted of the fact that he had been born in Maillane, the site of one of the very few archaeological discoveries anywhere near Hannibal's route which might have had some connection with his expedition. Towards the end of the eighteenth century, a man doing some building work on his cellar dug up what experts agreed was the skeleton of an elephant. True, Polybius insists that none of the elephants perished until the whole convoy was in Italy, but his claim can hardly be considered conclusive, or even likely, and the find has served (for two centuries so far) to fan still further the flames of Hannibalic controversy, the burning question being whether Hannibal's elephants were Indian or African. The man who found the skeleton found also a medallion with an elephant engraved on it, and fixed it to his pick; assuming that the medallion was of the same period as the elephant, and that both of them were of the same period as Hannibal, a sight of the pick would settle that argument for ever; unfortunately, the pick was lost. A glance at the bones would settle it, too, but they were lost as well. The carelessness of history has contributed in no small measure to the enduring nature of the Hannibalic argument.

A visit to the old Roman theatre of Arles was undeniably impressive, for all that it had been heavily restored and was now strewn with modern lighting, cigarette-butts and, of all things, hairpins. But the steep climb to the back was well worth it, though it raised in my mind a question that had often occurred to me before. In a city (Arles is one) with both an arena and a theatre, the theatre would be spared the necessity of putting on spectacular shows, with or without gladiators and animals; the equivalent of *Aladdin on Ice* would be given in the arena. What, then, was the normal repertoire of such a theatre? At Arles, as I looked down on the stage, I wondered whether this theatre played only the classics ('Seneca cannot be too heavy, nor Plautus too light'), or whether the audiences could also see the equivalent of trouser-falling farce. (A further, more alarming, thought: was that the function of Plautus? Did the actors' trousers fall down in the middle of the *Menaechmi* or *Miles Gloriosus*?)

A conversation with the *gardien* as I left raised another familiar question. Do I or do I not speak French? I have always believed that I do not; I can ask whether it has rained recently and compliment a lady on her new hat, but anything more profound, philosophical or linguistically complex is beyond me. And yet, once again – no, twice again – I demonstrated in Arles the extraordinary truth which every one who has only my wretched smattering of a foreign language knows, that *l'appétit vient en mangeant*. In the course of a day in Arles, I was engaged in two interviews in French, both of them with people who spoke not a word of English, and what is more, in one I was the interviewer and in the other the interviewed.

I was interviewed by the local radio station, which had heard of my Hannibal march, and wanted me to talk about it. But it was the interview in which I was asking the questions that provided one of the most memorable half-hours of the entire tour.

It was with Mme Dubocquet, who is the living image of the Van Gogh portrait known as *L'Arlésienne*. Mme Dubocquet keeps a little antique shop and is herself a native Arlésienne. A singularly charming one, too; her warmth would have softened my rage before the very *tricoteuses* of Orly. But in addition to being the Lady of Arles, and also being – as she plainly is – one of the world's leading experts on Van Gogh's life, she bears that extraordinary likeness. And that is not all; she received me dressed in a costume identical to that worn by Van Gogh's sitter, and I learned that the white silk *fichu* that she wore was the original, lovingly preserved. The whole extraordinary story came out; her mother had been a friend of the sitter's great-niece, who had inherited the scarf and given it to Mme Dubocquet. From this gift (my sitter was only a child at the time), an early interest in Van Gogh had become a lifelong passion. A passion, not an obsession; Mme Dubocquet was as balanced and sensible as she was charming, and she plainly revered the memory of the artist – she spoke with much wisdom of his madness, and of the tragedy that turned the world's first, unjust conclusion about him into terrible fact. Looking at her closely, I noticed that although she wore the costume of the painting exactly as the sitter did, she had not disguised her face or made herself up to heighten the resemblance; her features did genuinely bear a close likeness to those in the picture. (My first question had been whether she was herself related to the sitter: 'Malheureusement, non', she said.) She had been all over the world in search of Van Gogh knowledge, and worn the costume for television companies from England to Japan; the first time she went to Holland (for the opening of the Van Gogh Museum in Amsterdam), she was received by Theo's son, Vincent's nephew. I had the Van Gogh book on my lap, open at the picture, and glanced back and forth from page to woman as we talked; an experience which, had it not been so delightful, would have been disquieting.

Then to the drawbridge, which is perfectly preserved and instantly recognisable – a little more weather-beaten, naturally, but the very same. I could see how the artist had romanticised it with a roundedness and warmth that is not quite true; the bridge is more angular, harder, than he had painted and drawn it. Standing on the little road over the canal, which is only a few yards from the drawbridge, I could examine it in detail; it is presumably left open permanently now because that is what the visitor will expect to see.

Thus, as the green water crawled lazily underneath both bridges, I mused; and then came the old lady to spoil it all. She appeared with a shopping-basket; it transpired that she lived in the little house beside the bridge, and had done so for fifty years. And she insisted that it was not Van Gogh's bridge at all. That, she said, had been further down the canal, and had crumbled to bits long ago. Moreover (she was plainly enjoying herself), the fake that had replaced the original had been destroyed by a bomb during the war, and the one that I had been gazing at with all the appropriate emotions had been transported complete from another part of the canal.

Was I to believe my illusions or her? She sounded authoritative, though not expert (she knew none of the relevant dates). Perhaps she took delight in upsetting people; perhaps people had been upsetting *her*, knocking on her door to ask silly questions, with blue-rinsed American matrons demanding to know whether she was Mrs Van Gogh and whether she had her late husband's ear preserved under a glass bell on her mantelpiece. I thought of going back into Arles and asking Mme Dubocquet, but if she had repeated the crone's story I would have had to believe her. I decided to believe my illusions, and marched on.

Next day, I went to a Provençal bullfight, armed with the popular belief that in France the bull is not killed. Untrue, it seems; in the principal rings the distinction is kept, but in some of the little ones scattered about the area it is not. The police sometimes swoop on an illegal fight to the death, and the promoters are prosecuted, but the fines are so derisory they are counted as part of the overheads, and the practice continues unabated.

Anyhow, the bullfighting in Arles is always the bloodless kind, and that, I discovered, is by no means the only difference between the French and Spanish moment of truth.

The arena was packed; I was told it holds 20,000 people. A fanfare, then the band marched into the arena, playing *The Entry of the Gladiators*. The ringmaster was dressed in a gold cloak and a top hat; beneath the cloak he wore tails, and he had white gloves and carried a black stick. He led the band round the arena in a kind of ballet, while he leaped and capered in front of them. (The temperature in the shade was at least ninety degrees; on the sand it must have been well over a hundred.) After the band had completed their circuit they lined up beneath the President's box, and were followed by the ladies, beautifully and richly dressed, in costumes rather like that of my Arlésienne.

With the two bands and the *señoritas* in position, it was the turn of the horses – perfectly matched black ones, their riders dressed almost as colourfully as the ladies. At last came the matadors, dressed, to my astonishment, from head to foot in white, without a touch of colour. My helpful neighbour explained that they wore white rather than the traditional Spanish 'suit of lights' because they were not actually fighting the bulls at all, much less fighting them to the death. What, then, was the point? The point was their agility; the aim was for the matador to mark the bull by getting close enough to it to rake his hand over its back; on his hand he wore a curious instrument half-way between a gauntlet and a knuckleduster, and this, I learned, was to scratch the bull so that the lines would show up on its sleek coat and thus prove that the matador had touched it. He scored even more highly if he could snatch one of the rosettes fixed to the beast's flank.

Now everyone else left the arena, to more music, and the matadors – another surprise, their battle is a collective one, and there were about twenty of them altogether – faced the gate from which the bull was to emerge.

My helpful friend explained that the matadors are called *rassoteurs*, from the technique of scratching the bull's back, and at that moment from a door beneath me, the bull came galloping out, to stop in the middle of the arena, surrounded by a ring of white figures. From then on, it was gradually borne in upon me that Provençal bullfighting is extremely boring.

Back and forth darted the *rassoteurs*; every few moments the bull put down its head and ran at them, not very energetically, whereupon they all scattered for the barrier and leaped it, leaving the bull to trot back into the middle of the arena and begin the game again. Each bull is allowed fifteen minutes in the arena; a fanfare signals the end of the round and the bull trots out.

The second bull was bigger and much fiercer. From the start, he was plainly determined to get at the enemy, and his repeated rushes had them leaping for the barrier every few seconds. None of them was caught, but twice a *rassoteur* scored, and the marks of the scraper could be seen plainly on the bull's coat. The round ended with honours even, and cheers for both sides, with the bull getting an extra accolade in the form of an excerpt from *Carmen*. This seemed to me as good a moment as any to leave too, and I did so, feeling that the bulls which were to make up the rest of the programme would be much like those I had already watched perform.

What had I seen? An exhibition of considerable skill and agility on the part of the *rassoteurs*, and of vigour on the part of the bull. Why, then, had it been of so little interest apart from the parade at the beginning and the first few minutes of the fight itself? I considered, and rejected, the thought that it had been uninteresting precisely because the bull's blood had *not* been spilled, as circus audiences are said to be waiting eagerly for the trapeze artist to fall off the high wire and be dashed to pieces. I concluded that it was the lack of grace among the *rassoteurs*, nimble though they were, that had made the fight at Arles so unimpressive. But then, it is hardly for me to criticise those white-clad figures; I would not have gone into that arena with a spaniel, let alone a bull. With which reflection, I went off to visit the twelfth-century cloister of St Trophime.

A greater contrast with the arena and its sand, noise, heat and primitiveness could hardly be imagined. It was cool, simple, beautiful; on three sides the stone was absolutely intact, and on the fourth almost so, and the garden in the middle was plainly tended with love. The whole thing was tiny, not more than about twenty yards each side, the vaulted roof was without conscious grandeur – this was not King's College Chapel, after all – and the slim marble pillars at each corner were carved with friendly-looking saints. Outside, on the tympanum, there is a Last Judgment with the saved on one side and the damned on the other, but here, amid this contemplative calm, no such thoughts intruded; the atmosphere was of the Baroque, not the Middle Ages. If only, I thought, I could take it with me on my march; an hour pacing this little square would be the perfect antidote to the heat and labour of the day.

There was another element to the contrast between the arena and the cloister: not just Church and State, but ancient Rome and Christ. Julius Caesar was fond of Arles; Constantine IX, who made Christianity the official religion of the Roman Empire, built a palace there. But between Caesar and Constantine lay nearly four centuries, and the almost unimaginable gulf of those years can be sensed by a visit to the cloister after the arena; the contrast would be even starker if the tour were to be made the other way round. Christ got out of the dilemma politely: render unto Caesar ... We cannot square the circle so easily. We have to choose, and the choice is limited. Is the arena true, or is the cloister? The sport for which the arena was built; the trappings of Caesarism and Empire; the world, the flesh and the devil; these are still with us in their modern forms, and it is impossible and naive to think that we can wish them away. Facing them is the principle for which the cloister was built, offering its eternal and unchanging vision of another world. Black lamb and grey falcon; *le rouge et le noir*; even St Peter's rock and Constantine's absurd notion; the strain of attempting to reconcile the irreconcilable can be seen everywhere today, not least in those emptying churches in which, as David Lodge put it in his novel *How Far Can You Go?*, the congregation 'might find itself urged to pray for the return of someone's lost tortoise or the success of the Viet Cong'. Eventually, the Arles arena and St Trophime are held to be equally valid, and bullfighting almost indistinguishable from the Mass. For my part, I do not know whether St Trophime is true; but I am quite certain that the arena is false.

This problem is not altogether different from the Van Gogh problem, which I pondered on a detour to the similar little cloister that he must have paced a thousand times during his year in seclusion, undergoing treatment after his self-mutilation; the place remains a clinic for the mentally ill, and now bears his name. Today's fashionable view is that Van Gogh was perfectly normal, that his action in cutting his ear off was only his way of expressing himself, that to regard it as evidence of mental imbalance, let alone as suggesting that he needed skilled help, is to display bourgeois prejudice, and (if all else fails) that he was driven to it by the intolerable pressures of an outmoded Protestant work-ethic. The explosion of creative genius that took place in his year next to the cloister has almost no parallel anywhere in art; the heightened consciousness that was the result of his affliction can be measured not only by the genius but by the colours – unprecedented even for him – in which it poured out. The drawbridge and the fields of sunflowers were there for him to portray; the furnace of creation raging in him, however, is beyond our comprehension. Plainly, the mutilation and the canvases came from the same source of feeling, but the spring is too deep for us to sound. Van Gogh had nothing to do with the world (which never bought a single one of his pictures in his lifetime), though he acted as a conduit through which he filled his world and ours with astounding beauty. Would he have been better off, this Icarus who went too close to the sun, if he had spent his year in an arena rather than a cloister?

Leaving Arles, I discovered that it has a *rue* Robespierre; it would be a most unpropitious address. Fontvieille, the next stop, has a special claim to fame; beside it stands the windmill of Daudet, the very *moulin* from which he wrote the letters. I had not read him since I was a schoolboy, when I felt it was all very soppy, but I thought I owed him a re-reading. I then discovered that Daudet is far from the sentimental children's author I had supposed him. The tale of the young man who kills himself for love, and the one of the miller whose trade has fallen away because he refuses to use the new methods but whose pride will not allow him to admit that he has no work even though he is starving, are hardly *Little Women*: 'Those robbers, to make bread, use steam, which is an invention of the devil, whilst I work with the north and north-west winds, which are the breath of God.'

The road to Fontvieille led along another canal, this one much smaller than those of the Camargue, and its banks far more overgrown. It was rough underfoot, and I had almost to push my way among the foliage; beyond the track were cornfields of Van Gogh gold, which is not the yellow gold of the metal itself but the yellow, appropriately enough, of good wheaten bread. I am not enough of a countryman (I am *nothing* of a countryman) to know whether the corn I could see represented a good harvest; certainly, the fields seemed crowded to overflowing, but for all I knew the farmers were grumbling, as they prepared to cut it, at the niggardliness of nature. (The only exception to the grower's complaint of poor harvests is the man who tends the vines; wine-growers, in my experience, have always been cheerful souls, thanking God most warmly for sending them grapes in such abundance.)

The little track wound delightfully on; from time to time a lizard would scuttle across my boot, and occasionally there was a slithering noise in the bushes, made by something invisible but plainly larger than a lizard; it suddenly occurred to me that I did not know whether there were any snakes in this part of France, and if so whether they were the poisonous variety. There were certainly horses, for their hoofprints were constantly visible in the dusty ground, and they must have been here recently, because there were fresh droppings. (I suppose Hawk-eye, Last of the Mohicans, could have told from the hoofprints and the droppings what kind of horse had gone by, where it had come from and where it was going, and perhaps even who was sitting on it.)

Another mystery (my ignorance of nature is truly appalling); passing a field dotted with sunflowers I noticed that they were all turning their backs on the setting sun; I could only suppose – since I am naturally convinced that sunflowers always turn towards it (though I have never been able to work out how they manage to avoid strangling themselves as they follow it round the sky) – that they were going to sleep in that manner in order to be woken up by the rising sun. But this theory, in which I only half believed, promptly collapsed when I passed a field entirely filled with sunflowers, every one of which was staring straight at the sun. Perhaps sunflowers *en masse* face sunwards but those growing singly among other crops do not. But why should that be?

The canal had by now narrowed to little more than a trickle; as I passed a handsome old stone bridge – two arches and a little buttress in the middle – I saw the path into Fontvieille, and as I crested the hill the first sight to meet my eyes was the windmill itself, looking exactly like the illustration on the cover of my copy of Daudet that I remembered from my childhood. In the Hôtel Bernard, where I stopped the night, there were the usual posters and postcards and paintings of it, but I suddenly remembered the Cassandra of Arles, materialising at my elbow to deny authenticity to the Van Gogh drawbridge; was somebody going to tell me that the Daudet windmill was not the real one either? I went to bed without making enquiries; better not risk further disillusion.

I started out very early; the walk from Arles had been done in scorching heat, and I had no reason to suppose that the next stage would be any cooler, so the couple of hours before the sun was high would be welcome. I was rewarded almost at once with a fine sight; a man leading a huge herd of goats, at least a hundred of them, down the road and towards a field where they were presumably to be pastured. Two dogs brought up the rear, but as the mass of animals got nearer I saw that the herd was of sheep, not goats; there were only a few goats among the sheep (metaphors threatened on every side), and as they passed me I realised to my astonishment that the goats were acting as auxiliary dogs, chivvying the sheep along. Perhaps the whole scene was out of a fairy story – goats, usually as sinister figures, abound in such tales, and the dogs were both black, which reinforced the feeling that I was still asleep in my bed at the Hôtel Bernard; when I finally noticed that the goatherd himself carried a scythe, I was sure I must be dreaming, and it was as much as I could do not to wake up and call for coffee and croissants.

I found another canal, this one running parallel to the main road, the RN 570, laden with roaring traffic even before eleven o'clock; the canal was a couple of hundred yards away, in well-wooded country, so the traffic was hardly noticeable. On my canal-track there was no one other than an elderly lady on a bicycle, clearly taking her morning constitutional, and so surprised to see me that she nearly wobbled herself into the water.

Soon, orchards began to appear beside my track, and soon afterwards a farmer was a couple of apples short, followed by a peach. 'Scrumping', which is what it was called in my boyhood, used, I seemed to remember, to require a stone and a steady aim to bring the fruit down; here I hardly needed to raise an arm to pluck it. This could not be the familiar experience of the childhood home, revisited, looking so much smaller than it had been in the eye of memory; were apple-trees taller in my youth? Thinking about it, I realised that for many years I had seen no apple trees other than the small ones, mere bushes; perhaps they have been bred, over the years, into the compact size, as gooseberries have been persuaded to be hairless, though when I was a child they were always covered with a soft stubble.

Just inside a beautiful, and beautifully tended, field of what I at first took to be potatoes, but soon realised was sweetcorn, there was working a solitary figure; we said 'Bonjour' simultaneously, and he came to the edge of the field, clearly ready for a break. I crossed the path, and addressed him in my broken French; to my surprise, his was even more broken than mine, and it transpired that he came from Tunisia. I asked him if he had been in France for long – he must have been still in his twenties – and he said that he had only just arrived; he liked to wander from country to country, seeing the world and working his passage. I asked if he journeyed on foot, and he said of course, it was the best way of seeing the world. 'Mais vous aussi', he added, nodding at my rucksack. I guessed, but did not ask, that his belongings would probably fit into a pocket; immediately, there came to mind the legend of the ailing king whose doctors tell him that he will be cured only by wearing the shirt of a truly happy man. The king's emissaries are sent to scour the land for this paragon, but every claimant approached turns out to have some disqualifying worry or pain. Finally, when the king is at death's door, the court hears of a man who fulfils the condition exactly; alas, when they find him – laughing and singing – they discover that he is so poor he hasn't a shirt to his back.

I walked on thinking of my Tunisian friend – he had certainly seemed to have not a care in the world, though he did wear a shirt. I hitched my rucksack a shade higher, and began to think about its contents. If the young man had owned everything in it *but nothing else at all* he would, I guessed, have counted himself the possessor of a substantial inheritance. I knew that when my journey was over I would be going home to living conditions which to him would have been as the wealth of a Prince in a fairy-tale. Yet I am not a rich man, though I live in comfort, travel without hardship, and have to my back not just one shirt but dozens. Now the young man, and any wise philosopher, would point out that however many shirts a man owns, he can wear only one at a time; if the philosopher was observant as well as wise, he might also deduce that the Tunisian farm-labourer was happier than I. I have never been interested in the cliché that money does not buy happiness; it has too often led fools to the conclusion that the poor do not mind their poverty. The question is not 'What is it that clouds my serenity?' but 'What is the secret of the young man's unclouded kind?' Obviously, he found happiness inside him, not in his wardrobe, or in his larder, but that is practically a tautology: what lay inside his heart, and what enabled the man without a shirt to his back to laugh and sing all day, while the king wasted on his sickbed?

I rejoined the path beside the canal; while I was still wrestling with the question I spotted my shadow on the other bank. I recalled, on a visit to India, going up to Amber and being persuaded to do the journey, which was only a mile or so, on an elephant. I paid my rupees and climbed the ladder that led to the howdah; on the way to Amber I discovered that elephant-back was the most damnably uncomfortable mode of travel I had ever experienced. First of all the road was very steep and rocky. Second, I realised that an elephant has four legs and what might be called independent suspension for each of them; I remembered too late the peculiar character of the elephant's walk, which is that it raises each foot from the ground separately and slowly, and puts it down with great deliberation before the next mighty foot is lifted. That meant that on my ride I had four separate shocks and a tilt in four directions for every complete pace the animal took. Worse still was that the howdah in which I was sitting was a kind of box, rather like a square orange-box, and there was no way of getting comfortable in it. Obviously, I could not straddle the elephant's back as if it had been a horse (not that I could or would straddle a horse's), and there was therefore nowhere to put my feet; I had to hunch up my knees and simultaneously hold on to the sides of the orange-box as it swayed violently back and forth and from side to side while the elephant went on up with its quadripartite stride, and there was a very real possibility that a more than ordinarily vigorous lurch would throw me out and off; in addition, the bottom of the orange-box was uncovered and uncushioned, and very hard indeed.

The only consolation for that ride was that at one point, as we went round a bend, a shadow was thrown on the rock wall – a shadow consisting of an elephant with me sitting on its back, both of us life-sized and without any distortion; the sight was so striking and extraordinary that I felt I must take a photograph of it. (It did not come out; perhaps shadows cannot be photographed.) The whole weird experience was rounded off by an Indian who ran along beside the elephant playing a violin very badly indeed, and addressing the elephant's passenger as a Maharajah, in the hope that such flattery would be rewarded with cash. I got the idea fairly quickly and threw down some money; it was caught neatly, and I was addressed as Maharajah again before the violinist returned to the bottom of the path to start serenading the next unfortunate elephant-rider.

As I was thinking about my elephant-ride in India, and concluding that Hannibal must have been mad to want to travel on one, I kept eyeing my shadow nervously, perhaps for reassurance. The happy man in the story has no shirt, but a man or woman without a shadow is invariably, in legend, a woeful figure, doomed to unhappiness (as in Richard Strauss's *Die Frau ohne Schatten*, for instance, in which the woman's lack of a shadow represents her barrenness). My shadow, to my relief, never left me, and there was a bonus awaiting me; the canal went right into the town, so that I never had to join the road, now terrifying with the monsters that roared along it.

Tarascon is Daudet country, too; his Tartarin, with the dreams of Don Quixote but the soul of Sancho Panza, is another of that gallery of rogues who are constantly being worsted by fate, the law or greater rogues, but whom we love because of their faults rather than despite them; why is Falstaff held in such universal affection, and why do we prefer Parolles to all the unco guid around him in *All's Well that Ends Well*?

There seemed little evidence of Tartarin in Tarascon, where it was market day; he would never have felt at home in the castle, a stupendous pile in golden stone, perhaps a hundred feet high, with two massive round towers and a broad, deep moat – drained now, and rather prettily overgrown. Facing it across the river was Beaucaire and its own castle; when I crossed the bridge and got near to it I could see that Beaucaire Castle had only one wall and one tower standing, but when both fortresses were young they must have been an imposing and frightening sight – the river at this point marked the old border of Provence – to anyone venturing between them.

A visit to the church of St Martha was obligatory, not only for its engaging mixture of Romanesque and Gothic, but because of St Martha's adventures with the Tarasque, from which the city got its name. The Tarasque was a monster which lived in the Rhône in the eleventh century, popping out from time to time to pick up a passing cow for its dinner or a strayed child for its lunch. St Martha, the fame of whose piety had spread from her home at Ste Marie de la Mer as far as Tarascon (then presumably unnamed), was sent for. She stared disapprovingly at the monster, which quailed into docility at her glance, attached it to her girdle, and went about in that fashion from then on. Or so they say in Tarascon.

Some of the ancient walls of Tarascon are still standing, and I walked right through the little town to the fourteenth-century Porte de la Condamine; it was approached by the inevitable *rue* Jean Jaurès, though I discovered to my delight that Tarascon had done more than merely commemorate the celebrated Socialist: it had marked the object of his concern with a *rue* Proletariat. (I also found a *rue* Mirabeau. There is a *rue* Mirabeau in Aix-en-Provence, too, but they have more excuse – he sat for Aix in the États-Généraux.)

The market was at once a heartening and a depressing sight. Depressing because all the artefacts I could see were souvenirs of the vilest kind, heartening because the food was not only plainly local and plainly good, but displayed, however simply, with that extraordinary instinctive taste for colour and shape that the French seem to have. (In the smallest shop in the smallest town, if the assistant does up your package with ribbon, she will invariably run the ends of it, with her thumb, against one blade of the scissors, so that it curls prettily.)

There was a stall selling nothing but sausages – eleven varieties, perfuming the air – another which specialised even more narrowly, offering nothing but bulbs of garlic, another which sold only olives, green and black, large and small, smooth and wrinkled, another selling only honey, dark and light, thick and clear, yet another offering ground spices, forty or more, all arranged in little dishes on a long table like a giant palette.

Sausages and garlic, oil and spices, honey and fruit; something was missing. I found it at the edge of the market; it could get no closer to the centre because it was not a stall but a huge lorry with one side hinged along its entire length and lowered to form the table for a display of – I counted them – seventy-eight varieties of cheese; if the sausage-stall had scented the air, this filled it, and I lingered long by the array, breathing in the crisp sourness of the little goat-milk discs, the pungent warmth of the crumbly blues, the soft *pourriture noble* of the *tommes* and *vacherins*, the sweetness of the plain hard strains, which Britain does better than France.

Mad dogs and Englishmen go out in the midday sun. I crossed the river into Beaucaire for some lunch, and as far as I could see I was the only living creature stirring; there was not even a sleeping mad dog for me to tiptoe past, terrified that it might wake and bite me rabid. Every house had its shutters closed, every shop its door-blind drawn; I might have been in Ecclefechan on the anniversary of John Knox's death. But stay! there was a sound of bicycle wheels, and a small boy – he could hardly have been more than seven – came round the corner struggling with four gigantic loaves, taller than he was, to grace the family lunch. Just before he saw that he was not alone in the street he broke off a piece and stuffed it into his mouth. As he went by, I called out to him 'C'est bon?', but he only blushed furiously and pedalled off.

Beaucaire had much more unspoilt charm than Tarascon. Little ancient streets, with inhabited arches spanning them, were everywhere; in the window of one private house there was a sign reading 'Vente de canaris', and under it the announcement 'Dix francs les six'; nobody could have failed to respond appropriately: are not five sparrows sold for two farthings? The answer was: in Beaucaire not necessarily, but six canaries will cost you ten francs.

Napoleon slept here, or at least ate. A plaque on the wall of a tiny house showed a group of men at table and Napoleon entering the room. Beneath the frieze was a quotation that seemed to be from a diary. (Did he keep a diary? Presumably he did, if only to accommodate that feeble palindrome so implausibly attributed to him: 'Able was I ere I saw Elba'. Almost all palindromes are feeble, two exceptions being 'Dennis and Edna sinned' and the one on de Lesseps: 'A man, a plan, a canal – Panama!') The plaque said 'Je me trouvais à Beaucaire le dernier jour de la foire', and underneath it, 'Le souper de Beaucaire, 29 Juillet 1793'. Well, if he could eat in Beaucaire, so could I; Le Fiacre advertised *Salle climatisée*, and since the temperature was well into the nineties, that settled it. At the next table was a couple who greeted me in my own tongue, assuming that I was British; mad dogs ... or perhaps my crumpled shirt, my straw hat and my rucksack could belong only to that nation of eccentrics. We made polite conversation for a moment and the husband then gave me the astonishing and improbable news that York Minster had burnt down during the night. I thought I must

4 *At the helm of Captain Mimi's rowing-boat* 5 *Arles: at the café that Van Gogh painted* 6 *Cassandra voices her doubts* 7 *The drawbridge opens: the ghosts pass through* 8 *The very mill at which Daudet wrote the letters*

5

6

7

9

10

have misunderstood, but the wife repeated the claim in words which left no doubt. They even went into details; from these, fortunately, I learned that the building had been extensively damaged but not destroyed, and that the towers and the glass had survived.

York has always been my favourite among the English cathedrals, and the news was a blow; my mind at once leaped back sixteen years to an August day in a little Austrian inn, where I had been having breakfast on the morrow of my birthday and heard two men at the next table talking in earnest tones about something sensational that had happened. It was tantalising, because since they both knew what it was, they had no need to tell one another, and from their comments about it it was impossible for me to deduce its nature, particularly as my German is even weaker than my French. Then one of the men said, 'In my opinion the Poles won't stand for it', whereupon I could stand for it no longer: I abandoned my breakfast and went out to find a newspaper that would tell me what it was that the Poles would not stand for. It was the Soviet invasion of Czechoslovakia.

I recrossed the river, and as I did so a gust of wind snatched my hat from my head and sent it sailing down to the Rhône; it was an exact replay of my experience at Cape Sounion, and it was the very hat that I had bought to replace the one that Boreas had stolen on that occasion. Now I would have to repeat the purchase, too. As the hat landed in the water, I felt that the occasion warranted something more than a simple exit, so – since it was floating majestically along, borne up by the river – I improvised a speech, beginning 'Adieu, brave chapeau, compagnon de ma jeunesse', and a small crowd collected, clucking sympathetically; there were even helpful suggestions as to how I might retrieve it.

Having made such good time to Tarascon, I thought I would push on further, for a landfall a few miles along the road; had I been able to guess at the disaster that lay ahead of me, I would have been tempted to follow my hat into the river.

Another tiny canal, utterly deserted, with not a sound but my boots and the breeze stirring the trees. Then, abruptly, and in flat contradiction of the map, the canal vanished underground, never to be seen again, and the path beside it came to an end at the same time. On one side of me was the railway-line, guarded by an unclimbable fence; on the other the RN 570, now covered with traffic thundering past nose-to-tail in both directions at sixty miles an hour. For the moment, at least, there was a verge, a yard or so wide, so that, descending to the road (I had no other choice), I could get along it in conditions which

9 Following the sun round the sky   10-11 Two dozen varieties of olive . . . and four dozen spices

were unpleasant though not dangerous. But the sun was now beating down on me like a refiner's fire, and I found that I was dehydrating at an alarming speed. I remembered having read somewhere that it is not heat that kills people in deserts, it is the loss of fluid; I told myself that I was not in a desert but in a heavily-populated part of Western Europe, so that I was hardly going to die of dehydration; I could knock on a door and ask for water. Then I realised that I was walking along a road which had no buildings of any kind on either side, nor any turning off it. There was no door for me to knock at.

By now I was feeling extremely dizzy; what was to be done? I could not flag down a car from the flow of hurtling traffic, I could see no oasis ahead, and the hotel I had booked at was still some five or six miles away. To the dizziness there was presently added a most disagreeable shivering, and I began to contemplate the interesting possibility of dying, for when I collapsed unconscious by the roadside it would still be impossible for a car to stop and investigate, even if the driver realised that I was ill rather than taking a nap.

Far ahead, I saw a solitary building on the other side of the road; as I came closer I saw a sign on the wall facing me. I could make out only the first word, which was 'Relais'. Unless I was delirious, and this sight a mirage, I was saved, but just as that comforting thought struck me, I remembered the French habit of renting space on a wall to advertise a hotel or restaurant several miles further down the road. What if it was only such an advertisement that I was looking at, and what if the building was a deserted factory or school?

No, it was a Relais; I scuttled across the road, entered the deserted room and made a noise until a woman appeared. I asked her for the largest and coldest bottle of mineral water she had, and I then heard, but could scarcely believe, words which could only mean that in a perfectly ordinary bar in the middle of France *there was no mineral water*. Swaying, I demanded beer instead. I poured two litres down my throat at a go; it had no effect at all, and only as I got to the end of the third litre did I feel that I had got past the point of simply replacing the liquid I had lost.

Next morning I equipped myself with a plastic flask, and never again did I set out on a day's march without knowing that it was in my rucksack, and filled.

A good night's sleep, preceded and followed by another gallon or so of mineral water, restored me, though I had a nasty moment while waiting for the hotel bill to be made out and, glancing round the lobby, found it dominated by a huge photograph of Frédéric Mistral, his hat and cravat floppier than ever. I struck off across the fields and eventually found a tiny road that was plainly taking me where I wanted to go. The trouble with striking off across the fields, however, is that it leads the traveller past isolated farmhouses, and isolated farmhouses mean dogs. And at least seven times out of ten, dogs mean Alsatians.

I dislike almost all dogs, but Alsatians, I do truly believe, should be prohibited by law in any civilised country. They are *always* untameable; not a week goes by without one of them turning against its owners and causing frightful injuries, very often to children. Not only are they untameable, but what makes it worse is that most of the fools who buy one believe that all they have to do is to take it home and feed it; it does not seem to cross their minds that some kind of training is necessary when there is a literally lethal instrument on the premises. Again and again, on this tour, I was passing a house, going nowhere near the property, when one of these savage and repulsive animals leaped out, yelling and snarling and snapping at me. One day, I promised myself, I would reverse my stick and bring the thick part down on the beast's head with all the force I could put into the action. For obvious reasons, I would have to stun or disable it with that first blow.

The more I see of dogs, the more I admire men. Leaning over a gate was a genial-looking soul, clearly too well-balanced to be a dog-lover, who was spending the morning watching life go by. I greeted him, and he replied 'Je vous fais un vent pour vous pousser' – not only a generous thought but a lively phrase. I stopped for lunch at a Relais Routier in Rognonas; we are so used to thinking of these as simple restaurants for the tourist – which indeed they are – that we tend to forget what the words mean, but I could not have forgotten here; in a sleepy little village, on a weekday, there were twenty-three men in the room, and as far as I could tell I was the only one who was not a *routier*; the lorries were parked outside in an immense row. I paused before leaving to telephone for a room at a hotel listed in my *Guide des auberges* as 'Odette et Patrick'; a woman's voice said, snappishly, 'C'est l'Hôtel Odette'. Did this, I wondered, imply some marital rupture? The voice had been snappish, mind, not grieving; clearly Patrick was not dead, but gone before. There was no opportunity to find out, however, as Odette had no vacancy, apart, presumably, from the one left by Patrick.

What with the Relais Routier, and the man who wished me a wind to blow me on my way, and the dramatic story of Odette and Patrick, I swung cheerfully into Avignon, through those implausible walls, and left my rucksack at the station before setting off to explore the town.

The Rhône –
M. Mousset's Wine and
M. Breton's Bottles

AVIGNON EPITOMISES the dilemma of tourism; it has been more comprehensively ruined by visitors than any other originally beautiful city I know. The whole place looked as though it had decided that since the Popes would not be returning Avignon had better make the best, or rather the most, of what it could get. Obliged to wade breast-high through litter, I studied the contents of it: the debris of take-away hamburgers and fried chicken, together with empty soft-drink tins, predominated, though discarded newspapers formed a surprisingly large proportion of the whole (they may be dirty in Avignon, but at least they know what is going on in the world), and there was an astonishing quantity of leaflets advertising the fringe theatrical events of the Festival. These numbered dozens, perhaps scores – in a few minutes' walk along the main thoroughfare I had at least fifteen thrust unsolicited into my hands. (Edinburgh, where the fringe numbers several *hundred* events, has the same problem, but in Edinburgh they sweep the litter up.)

One of the theatrical entertainments I was bidden to was called *Onanisme avec troubles nerveux chez deux petites filles*; the trouble with that kind of title is that by the time the prospective customer has read it he feels he knows as much about the play as he would if he were to sit through it, like those headlines in *Nice-Matin* which relieve the reader of the necessity of reading the story below them: I remember one which went *Un bras d'homme dans une décharge publique – mauvaise plaisanterie?* and another that announced *Un bébé (4 ans) avale une hypodermique chirurgicale: il est évacué sur Marseille par hélicoptère.*

There was a perceptible hardness about Avignon; the waiters in the cafés, the shopkeepers, the people bumped into on the pavements. That is what I meant by the ruin that tourism brings; the hardness came from a town that hates the visitors and simultaneously despises itself for needing them. No doubt the tourist season in Avignon, as in so many resorts all over the world, is short; the natives must gather their rosebuds while they may. But since such places, after a time, attract only the least discerning visitors, who also tend to be the least considerate, the result is to divide the people there into those who arrive resolved to make it a bigger mess than it already is and those already in position who are determined to make the visitors pay for their grim pleasure in discomfort as well as money.

Tourism is the inescapable plague of our times. Almost every country in the world (Burma is a notable exception) encourages it; since the end of the Second World War it has become one of the world's greatest industries, and the economy of some countries could not survive its loss. Yet the price paid is always, in the end, higher than anything gained in the way of hard currency. In the areas that sustain the heaviest incursions, the restaurants sell the worst and cheapest food and drink they think they can get away with, the shops are full of souvenirs indistinguishable from souvenirs all over the world, and in the wake of the tourists, like the camp-followers of an invading army, come the hangers-on and the hopeless, the bums and the beggars. The able-bodied beggars in Avignon were among the most brazen I have ever seen; some of them strummed a guitar and sang a few verses before passing the hat around, but some didn't even bother to do that; I could not sit for ten minutes at a café table before seeing a young man, without giving even the pretence of anything in return, shove a tin tray in the faces of customers, demanding coin.

One or two of these subsistence-farmers gave value; the artists who undertook, like their opposite numbers in the courtyards of the Uffizi in Florence, to draw the passer-by in charcoal for a modest sum would never get into even the Royal Academy Summer Exhibition, but I came upon one who was doing caricatures of his sitters instead of the earnest portraits that most of his rivals offered, and I succumbed to his appeal. As he sketched, he told me that he was Iranian, a student now living in Paris; he came here in the holiday season to earn a little money. He was neither deferential nor surly – the two most common characteristics of those who live too long by tourism – and he had some talent; his version of me was amusing, more or less accurate, and even recognisable. I paid him with good grace, which is more than I did with the waiter who swore at me for moving my chair.

The first sight of the Palais des Papes was very impressive; as I came into the square it loomed over me like a huge castle – towers, turrets, battlements and all. I had not seen it for many years, and had quite forgotten how vast it is; strictly speaking, it is not one Palais but two, and the 'join' of the two architectural styles is plainly visible. The Popes of Avignon were plainly not going to risk any unfavourable comparisons with Rome, and built on this scale so that no one who knew how the other half lived would be able to smile at them. But that was by no means the most extraordinary thing about the Great Schism.

What was, I wonder – apart, obviously, from the theological differences themselves? I sometimes think it was the influx of Cardinals into Villeneuve-lès-Avignon on the other side of the river; when the papal entourage filled Avignon, the Cardinals decided that it would be wiser not to try to find space for their own establishments under the papal windows, and decamped across the bridge. Villeneuve at that time was hardly more than a sleepy little village; abruptly awoken, it must have thought itself still dreaming, for eventually there were no fewer than fifteen scarlet-clad Cardinals, each with his palace and his people, and the streets must have looked as though they were perpetually awash with blood. But my favourite picture in all the years of the division of Christendom is the rise of a *third* claimant to the throne of St Peter, the false John XXIII, who lives in history because of the sentence in which Gibbon recorded his ultimate fate: 'The most scandalous charges were suppressed; the Vicar of Christ stood accused only of piracy, murder, rape, sodomy and incest.'

The bridge across which the bishops decamped must have been the Pont St Bénézet, which is the one the song is about; the bridge is now a stump, its four remaining arches presumably representing a hazard to river traffic, but the charm remains. I lingered long on it, contemplating the smart but soulless replacement a couple of hundred yards away, as well as the outline of the Palais des Papes, which crowns the horizon. The official theatre of this year's Avignon Festival included *Richard III*, so sold out that all I could get in the way of a place was permission to sit on a step in one of the aisles. It was given in the courtyard of the Palais des Papes, and pretty dire it was, starting with the translation. I wish the French would leave Shakespeare alone altogether; their inability to come to terms with him is typified by the fact that there are no translations that are even half tolerable. The famous Gide *Hamlet* is in fact ludicrous, and the modern one used for this *Richard III* was sorry stuff:

> Qu'on me donne un autre cheval! Qu'on bande mes blessures!
> Aïe pitié Jésus! du calme, ce n'était qu'un rêve.
> O lâche conscience, comme tu me tortures ...

The truth is that the French can no more comprehend Shakespeare than the English can Racine; but at least the English mostly leave Racine alone, thank God.

The production was in the now threadbare 1970s' style, very reminiscent of the Chéreau *Ring*; inventive, but the invention consistently pointless. Lady Anne, for instance, brings on the body of the dead Henry (which is a rag doll) in a pram, and Clarence's murderers are dressed as a double-act of 1920s' *apache* dancers. Queen Elizabeth was played by a man, and in the scene in which Richard first refuses the crown and then accepts it, his entourage went off singing (in English) the old hymn 'The day thou gavest, Lord, is ended'. Act One ended with a mimed scene of Richard's Coronation, played in strobe lighting, an ancient trick that works now only when it is used by a genius, as it was when Lyubimov used it in his production of *Crime and Punishment*. I am now always terrified, ever since I read somewhere that stroboscopy in a theatre can set off an epileptic attack, that people will start having fits all round me where it's being used; I must say that I would have welcomed such a distraction at this performance. (Earlier on my walk I had seen a man having an attack of that strange malady, so long regarded, in so many cultures, as holy; he had fallen off his bicycle when the seizure took him, and I ran across the road to him, hanging on to my knowledge that the belief that it is necessary to fish an epileptic's tongue out of his throat is a myth, and a potentially lethal one. I put his saddlebag under his head and wondered what to do next, but his wife suddenly appeared – he had been struck down at his own garden gate – and took well-practised charge.)

Next day, I crossed over to Villeneuve to visit an 'artists' colony', itself a phrase redolent of the Twenties and the Left Bank and fierce arguments about André Breton in cafés with names like 'La Brebis qui Tousse'. This one was beautifully set in a fourteenth-century Carthusian monastery; it was arranged round the main church and a tiny, serene chapel. The artists in residence got a guaranteed income of £10,000 a year, with a very attractive little studio flat; including visitors, there were painters, sculptors, writers, people who did weird things with sound-mixers, a man whose work consisted largely of cabbalistic calculations – real ones, with the real Cabbala; there were exhibitions and performances and demonstrations. The question is, of course, what did it all amount to? And the depressing answer was that it amounted to no more than art ever amounts to when somebody announces 'Let there be art'. Money, studios, the peaceful and beautiful surroundings of the Villeneuve Charterhouse – it all made no difference, for Stravinsky was right when he said 'Nothing is certain about masterpieces, least of all whether there will be any.' The most depressing sight I saw (and there was much to choose from in the way of depressants) was a work on display in the original Chapter House – which was, incidentally, very well preserved, the walls decorated with some of the stone carvings that had been found or dug up when the place was being converted. These figures looked impassively down on a heap of very fine red sand in a pyramidical shape, with a bit of string tied to the vaulting of the building at the top and to the stone on the floor, running down just above the top of the pyramid; a series of eight or nine smaller heaps of the same-coloured sand lay along one wall. A notice at the door said that the work to be seen within was 'a non-object making a comment on time and space', which should have been warning enough. Unfortunately, the wretched lack of any true artistic impulse was cruelly accentuated by the beauty and simplicity of the surroundings. The men who built this tiny stone room, and those who did the carvings, certainly didn't think of themselves as artists at all, and perhaps that is the clue. You can set up an *artists'* colony in Villeneuve-lès-Avignon, and summon *artists* to it, and cook them all slowly in a large pot specially designed for cooking *artists*, and stir the *artists* mixture until the handle breaks off the spoon, but there is, and can be, no guarantee that anything that comes out of the pot will be ART. No one can create art by wanting to; no one can ask anyone else to create art with any serious hope of fulfilled expectations. It comes, always spontaneously at first, from inside an artist, and it never comes, or can come, in any other way. I have rarely seen that truth better demonstrated than at this sad, lovely place.

On the way out of Villeneuve, I passed the *rue* Gérard Philippe, Comédien: I have always thought this to be an odd word for an actor, and more so than usual in the case of Gérard Philippe. He was a very good actor; I saw him as Becket in the Anouilh play, in Paris, in the days when an annual visit to Paris was essential for any serious theatre-lover.

My route to Sauveterre lay up-hill, and a particularly steep hill it was; moreover, I made the mistake of allowing myself to feel encouraged, on entering the village, at the sight of a sign announcing the news that the Hostellerie de Varenne was 500 metres further on. Lies, wicked lies, as are all such tempting invocations to the weary traveller, who in this case had to trudge for fully twice the distance before the hotel came into view.

The view it came into was spectacular, and I had the best of it from my bedroom window, overlooking the hotel's terrace, its formal garden, the fields beyond, and the hills beyond those, now striped with giant shadows thrown by the setting sun. When it had finished setting, I drew back into the room, and began to think about the hotel. Clearly, it had once been a noble mansion, whether built by the nobility or those who had heard and taken to heart Thiers' famous exhortation: 'Enrichissez-vous!' The terrace below me must once have echoed with music and laughter, glittered with jewellery, livery and powdered wigs, looked out over many hectares of the owner's property. I changed, and went down on to the terrace for a drink before dinner, and after dealing with a mad kitten that was convinced it was a tiger and tried to prove the point by eviscerating my ankle, I fell to thinking about the building. It was not the first of the Hôtels du Tourisme I had stayed at on my march, and it was not to be the last; but I had already begun to see what they all had in common, and the sadness the reflection induced had nothing to do with the change of the house from a private and permanent dwelling to a commercial and transitory one.

These hotels are all, as far as inspection can reveal, struggling to survive. They have only a few rooms – this one had not more than a dozen or so – and they are all shabby; in my room, with its immensely lofty ceiling, there were cobwebs in the corners, and the carpets, though clean, were worn, the wallpaper, though not peeling, was faded (as well as hideous), and the wardrobe contained only a few wire coat-hangers.

It was easy to see from this example what had happened to such hotels in general; because their profit-margins were – must have been – shaved dangerously thin, they had no money to smarten themselves up, to replace curtains and furniture, to install telephones in the bedrooms or baths in place of showers in the bathrooms. But without such improvements, the ironclad French hotel regulations would not permit them to raise their prices, and without such improvements their ability to attract a regular clientele had declined. Thus caught simultaneously on both prongs of a new Morton's Fork, they had found themselves impelled by its jabbing to enter upon a downward spiral of decline leading to further decline. How many of these places had gone out of business altogether over the years I had no means of telling; but I was sure that if I were to repeat my journey exactly, five years hence, a good many of my nightly refuges would not be there.

Such gloomy thoughts vanished next morning when, soon after I started out, I paused to consult my map, and a helpful passer-by asked if I was looking for the Maison de Jeunesse. The cheerful mood induced by that encounter was brutally cut short. Coming down from Sauveterre and making for Châteauneuf-du-Pape, the only way across the river without a vast detour was the big suspension bridge that ran beside the one that carried the autoroute. Traffic on it was very heavy, but I could see that it had a pedestrian pavement on each side. Half-way along, I heard a curious high-pitched screaming, which at first I took to be the sound of a gull. I looked round for the bird, and could see none; the noise began again, and I realised that it was no bird, but something four-footed, and seemed to be coming from beneath my feet. I moved back and forth until I located its source, which was clearly on the girders beneath the bridge, and my next thought was that a puppy, which by then I realised must be the creature making the sounds, had fallen off the edge of the footwalk and landed a yard below on the metal supporting strut. A glance through the gap, however, made clear that that could not be the explanation, because the struts, which were set only a yard or so apart, sloped gently upwards to the pavement, so that even the youngest puppy could easily have trotted up one of them to safety. I took off my rucksack and knelt down, twisting my head until I could see through the gap at the right angle; when I realised what I was looking at I came close to being sick. It was a plastic bag, tied securely at the neck, and it was wriggling; I immediately realised that it contained not one puppy but several. Clearly, someone had put them in the bag to throw them into the river and drown them; either his throw had been too weak to clear the bridge altogether, or a gust of wind had blown the bag back as it fell, so that it had landed on the ledge. It was impossible to reach far enough to touch the bag from the pavement, and no one but an expert in a safety harness could have climbed down to it; the heat of the day was very fierce – I could hardly touch the metal of the bridge without discomfort – and the animals were certainly going to die very soon. Well, they would have died if the bag had fallen into the river as it had presumably been intended to. I walked on, disquieted by the cruelty that had condemned the animals to so horrible a death, and more so by my helplessness. I did not know whether there was any French equivalent of the RSPCA, and if so what it was called, and I greatly doubted if there was a branch in a town as small as Châteauneuf; I could not believe that the police could be persuaded to take an interest in the fate of an unwanted litter of puppies, I did not suppose I could find a steeplejack who might have the necessary equipment, and I realised in any case that by the time *any* rescue plan could be organised and put into effect the animals would be dead from natural causes. Ashamed of myself for finding comfort for my conscience in that thought, I walked on. But it was days before I ceased to hear that squealing sound.*

'Ici commence les célèbres vignobles de Châteauneuf-du-Pape'; this proud sign stood beside the road about a mile and a half outside the town, and the imposing ruins of the castle itself could be seen clearly astride the ridge on the horizon. (There must be a splendid view from it, but the path wound up a little too steeply to be inviting.) On both sides of the road stretched huge vineyards; I looked forward to sampling the result, because there are few wine regions in France or anywhere else which can equal Châteauneuf's boast that although it may not produce any great wines, it produces no bad ones at all.

More signs: mostly the names of the *domaines*, but one was advertising 'Circuit touristique', and it had been placed by the Fédération du Syndicat des Producteurs de Châteauneuf-du-Pape; that suggested that they took the visitor on a tour of the vineyards, doubtless offering him samples at every stop, so that he would inevitably end up the worse for wear. I was planning to confine my sampling to one *domaine* only – that of M. Louis Mousset's Château des Fines Roches; I did not then know that I would end up so completely the worse for wear that I would be provoked into coining a word for my condition: *déjambé*.

I stayed at the 'Chambre d'hôte' of Mme Melchor, where I was at once introduced to her little daughter, Marie; I have found throughout my life that very small children are always struck dumb on meeting me, even when (as in Marie's case) their parents assure me that they are normally incessant chatterboxes, and I could not persuade Marie to

---

*The first person to read the typescript of this book remarked that in thinking myself helpless to save the puppies, I had acted feebly. On reflection, I think he was right.

utter a sound. Perhaps my face is so alarming a sight (surely I would have heard about it if it were so?) that the children are terrified; more likely, this is one of the hazards of being a bachelor, the psychological differentness of one who has no children of his own being somehow instinctively apparent to a child; most likely of all, children can recognise a champion chatterbox, in whose company no child could hope to get a word in, so that they decide at the sight of me that they may as well fall silent and listen.

That evening I dined with M. and Mme Mousset; I had learned that they did not live at the Château, having found it too public, with strangers walking into their private apartment and demanding *dégustation*; but it was at the Château that, on the morrow, my own *dégustation* was to take place.

The Château des Fines Roches is not only an architectural fake; it is a fake so preposterous that I could not understand how the builders had ever finished their work, as they must have been helpless with laughter most of the time. From the other side of the valley, which was how I approached it, it looked mysterious and imposing, perhaps twelfth- or thirteenth-century. From closer, it could be seen to be mid-nineteenth-, and from closer still the very worst kind of mid-nineteenth-century design. First, it had been built from stone that simply wouldn't weather; it looked as though it had just come out of the box the shop had packed it in. Second, it was not only generally a fake; within the generality there were particulars – some of the towers, for instance, were only façades, like the streets in a Hollywood Western, and from behind could be seen to be entirely flat. It reminded me of that terrible period of late Victorian and Edwardian building in London, when the builders had discovered classical architecture, and in particular the fact that the columns of the Parthenon and similar buildings were very slightly convex, because if they had been perfectly regular they would have *looked* concave. What had escaped the English builder in his excitement at this new-found knowledge was that the Parthenon's columns swelled perhaps half a degree in a height of eighty feet, and the consequence was that the villas they built had columns which bulged by perhaps five degrees in ten feet; you can still see houses in parts of Kensington with a porch held up by a pair of columns that look like beer-barrels.

They do not look like M. Mousset's barrels, which were the size of houses, holding 5,000 litres each; I counted thirteen of these monsters, and even they were small compared to the metal vats in which the wine was fermenting. Over everything there hung that wonderful musty smell that the processes of wine-making invariably produce; I had heard that it can make you drunk if you do nothing but breathe it in for an hour or so, without touching a drop.

Jacques Mousset represents the fifth generation of his family to make wine here. He told me that he owned five vineyards, four classified as Châteauneuf-du-Pape and a fifth which lay just outside the area and therefore could not carry the name; total production was some 150,000 bottles a year. The four Châteauneuf wines are the Château des Fines Roches, the Domaine du Roi, the Font du Roi and the Clos St Michel; they were all poured with a steady and a generous hand by my host; he and his cellar-master and M. Bastier, who looks after the export side of the business, tasted it in the traditional way – a sip rolled round the mouth, then spat into a sawdust-lined bucket. I, true to my principle that if you are eating and drinking something good you should always remember the possibility that the world might come to an end before another hour has passed, decided to swallow rather than spit.

All four of the wines were very big and fruity; to my palate, it was the Font du Roi that was the biggest of them all, at least in its 1978 dress. Mousset himself proved to be a man of great quality and charm, with an almost Gascon panache; he spoke with real and affecting emotion about his life of wine, and even more so about the pleasure, the nobility, of this extraordinary thing. I was struck by the way in which he gently but very carefully made clear that he did not think that getting drunk on wine was either a pleasurable or a commendable activity; wine was something to be respected as well as enjoyed. His wife was very beautiful.

Châteauneuf-du-Pape was worth exploring, I found (I mean the town this time, though it was hardly more than a village), particularly since the first sight I saw in it was that of a group of five men, most of them elderly, sitting on a long bench up against the wall of a café, beneath the blackboard on which the simple menu was chalked. They only just fitted on to the bench, and they were laughing and joking and reminiscing. Again I recalled, as I had done in St Gilles, the Marcel Pagnol trilogy; these old men, enjoying life in the sunshine, meaning no harm, and watching the world go by, could have been straight out of *Fanny, Marius* or *César*.

Wine seemed to be pouring from every doorway, so many offers of *dégustation* and *vente* were there; *chez* Mousset there had been a constant stream of customers going in and out of the retail shop, many of them carrying those massive *bidons* which must hold a gallon at least. (In Châteauneuf one of the doorways actually was a barrel, set endways on.) As I left the town, with the vineyards all around me, planted in those guardsmen-straight rows, I still could not understand how and why vines flourish in what looks like soil too barren to sustain a cactus; some of them, indeed, were set straight into pebbles, like the surface of Brighton beach. I had heard the slogan 'the poorer the soil the better the wine', but I remained baffled. In among the vines was a solitary tree, the earth around it less inhospitable than the stony, chalky, sandy soil of the vines, and I made for it; a few minutes later, my stick standing upright in the earth with my hat sitting on it, and my head on my rucksack, I was fast asleep in its shade. It was a wise precaution, as well as being necessary for a man intending, that very evening, to sit through one of the longest operas outside Wagner: *Don Carlos*. My last thought but one as I sank into oblivion was that although it was not particularly odd that a town should be called 'The Pope's new castle' I had still never discovered how that twentieth-century Italian composer called Castelnuovo-Tedesco got *his* name, which means 'the new German castle'. Last thought of all was that the seats in the arena at Orange were of unyielding stone; I must somehow acquire a cushion before I go. No bad dreams disturbed my wine-dark sleep.

I awoke refreshed, and took the road to Orange, thinking about Jacques Mousset's life-filled philosophy of wine, and of the noble drink itself. It is one of the oldest of all human creations; the ancient Egyptians, six thousand years ago, drank wine, and Homer is full of it – indeed, the word always translated 'wine-dark' (the wine-dark sea), which he invariably uses when he wants to describe the purple colour the sea can achieve in the Aegean, must have been familiar when he used it, or the metaphor would have failed in its effect.

Hannibal's baggage-train had plenty of it, and even to them it was one of the oldest of the works of man's hand. Periclean Athens drank wine in much the same spirit as Jacques Mousset; we know of no culture, with a climate and soil in which the cultivation of vines was possible, that failed to produce wine. The literature of the world is full of wine, the images and metaphors of wine strew all the languages of the world, wine has sustained man ever since it was discovered (no one can say which of the three great blessings – bread, cheese, wine – came first), and it is surely no accident that so many of the great religions of the world incorporate wine into their most sacred rituals.

Wine, taken in moderation, makes life, for a moment, better, and when the moment passes life does not for that reason become worse. Christ's first miracle celebrated that fact (though St Paul did his best to spoil the effect later by saying 'Take a little wine *for thy stomach's sake*', a very nasty reason for drinking it), and the Christian churches have wisely responded by symbolically drinking Christ's blood in wine. Chesterton talked good sense on the subject:

> Feast on Wine or fast on water,
> And your honour shall stand sure;
> God Almighty's son and daughter,
> He the valiant, she the pure.
> If an angel out of Heaven
> Brings you other things to drink,
> Thank him for his kind attention,
> Go and pour them down the sink.

It was tea and (more particularly) cocoa that he had in mind, but he might well have included all alcoholic drinks other than wine, for they all (with the exception of brandy, which is really wine anyway) seem only feeble substitutes for the real thing. Belloc talked a great deal of nonsense on the subject of drink of all kinds, though he did once manage to say the right thing on the right subject, not in his *Heroic Poem In Praise of Wine*, which is horrible fustian, but in a much slighter poem:

> The wine they drink in Paradise
> They make in Haute Lorraine.
> God brought it burning from the sod
> To be a sign and signal rod
> That they who drink the blood of God
> Shall never thirst again.

But perhaps M. Mousset of Châteauneuf-du-Pape should have the last word. I asked him why we drink wine, and he replied with a speech of such delight that it deserves to remain in the original:

> Par amour du vin. Parce qu'on aime le vin. Moi, j'aime le vin, parce que le m'apporte la joie, le bonheur, la joie de vivre. Et en plus c'est mon métier, donc j'aime le vin. Faire simplement du vin, c'est possible, mais il faut le boire aussi, pour pouvoir l'aimer vraiment.

The northern gate to Orange (entering from the south, I had to traverse the city to see it) is the triumphal arch put up in honour of Julius Caesar, who was long dead when it was built; it was the Julian legions that took Orange, and the tradition of the chief must have been still strong in their ranks. Hannibal versus Caesar ... there, I reflected, would have been one of the greatest contests of the world; Hannibal finally succumbed to Scipio, but by then he was labouring under so many handicaps that his defeat was inevitable. The young Caesar and the victor of Cannae would have been evenly matched.

The arch was certainly a fitting memorial. Badly restored on one side, the other has been wisely left alone, and its huge central opening (two elephants could go through it side by side without difficulty) must have been a brave sight as the Roman soldiers marched into the city by way of dedicating it. Ave, Caesar ... Vive l'Empereur ... How did Hannibal's troops greet their commander? They didn't: for one thing, they had no common language, and for another, Hannibal was never interested in ceremonial parades.

I believe I am right in saying that no performance in the amphitheatre at Orange during the annual festival has ever started at the advertised time or within half an hour of it. Nonetheless, I felt obliged to be in my place as though I did not know that, and was rewarded for my unnecessary punctuality by a view of French chaos at its best. Used as I am to the opera mainly in Britain, in Germany and Austria, in the United States, I am used also (even in Italy) to tickets that explain clearly where the holder is to sit, to usherettes who are familiar with both the tickets and the seating, and above all to an orderly and quiet entry. A full half hour passed as new arrivals claimed the places the earlier comers were sitting in, with the usherettes, called in as umpires, unable to give any rulings. All over the vast bowl of the amphitheatre, I could see and hear arguments among different schools of thought concerning interpretations of the information on the tickets, and despairing cries from those, newly arrived ('Aux tard-venus les os'), who were wandering in the aisles, like tormented spirits seeking burial; their cries were addressed to those already seated along the rows, who might call back to them the numbers of the empty seats the lost ones had spotted, which numbers might in turn correspond to the numbers on their tickets, or, if not, might be interpreted, after a series of mystical and numerological calculations, as being in some symbolic way equivalent to them.

As the chaos showed little sign of ending, I had leisure to examine the theatre itself. Built just before the birth of Christ (while Virgil was writing the *Aeneid*), it was a triumphant statement of the Roman *imperium*, untroubled by any doubt, let alone by any prescience of the challenge that would soon be rocking the world. The facing wall, behind the stage, towered over the entire amphitheatre, looking for all the world as though it was the front wall of a mighty castle. From the stage before it, there flowed upward, in an unbroken wave, the tiers of seats, until the wave broke against the colonnade that ran round the back of the theatre. The backdrop itself was dominated by a mighty statue of Augustus, in whose reign the theatre was built; it was discreetly floodlit, and must have shaken the confidence of many an opera singer, conscious of its 'wrinkled lip and sneer of cold command' hanging over the stage.

The merry scene was interrupted for a moment by the arrival of ex-President Giscard d'Estaing, led to his seat (which by some happy accident turned out to be the right one) by an official of the management. Giscard's appearance was the signal for a demonstration and counter-demonstration – one group booing him and a rival faction applauding; the boos clearly had it, but that may be because booing will always be audible through clapping, and indeed through cheers (one of the few phenomena known to me that support the Manichee's case). How long ago, I thought, seemed the Giscard years, when the President would go shooting with his mad and murderous friend the Emperor Bokassa. No doubt Giscard was wont to dismiss with a Gallic shrug Bokassa's habit of exterminating his opponents in large batches and keeping bits of them in a refrigerator to provide an occasional midnight snack; possibly he would disarm his critics by saying that Bokassa was a rough diamond. I remember thinking, at the time of the French Presidential election in which Mitterand defeated Giscard, that if I had been a French citizen, I would have had considerable difficulty in deciding how to vote. On the one hand, the whiff that was by then being given off from the incumbent administration was enough to make even the less sensitive nostrils twitch; on the other, Mitterand's dubious political past and the much more than dubious political present of his alliance with the Communist Party hardly offered a promising future for either France or Europe, let alone NATO. I think I would have felt obliged to vote for Giscard, holding my nose as I did so. But how wrong I would have been!

From the first, Mitterand showed himself to be not only among the staunchest supporters of NATO, but quite explicit on the reasons for its necessity; in his unqualified denunciations of Soviet ambitions he caused grave offence among his Communist allies (in France the Communist leadership has always been unwaveringly Stalinist), but his willingness to offend them was widely attributed to the fact that since he had a majority in the National Assembly without their votes, he could if necessary do without them. And no doubt he had indeed come to that conclusion; what nobody foresaw, or could have foreseen, was that he must have planned from the start his astonishing achievement of single-handedly destroying the French Communist Party altogether as an effective, or even influential, political force. It was true that in Marchais, the PCF's leader, he had an ally; a stumbling brute, with neither tactical nor strategic sense, Marchais led his party into one cul-de-sac after another, swallowing every scrap of poisoned bait Mitterand held out to him, and incapable of contributing to France's political debate anything but incessant repetition of his mantra: the Soviet Union is always right.

Simultaneously, Mitterand, having started his rule by attempting to put into practice the ruinous economic policies he had advocated during the election, switched into sense so abruptly that even I, never much given to believing in the Machiavellian subtlety of politicians, began to wonder whether he had not planned that, too, from the start, continuing on the road to ruin only as long as he needed to justify adopting measures that he had always intended to put into practice but could not campaign on. There was a rumour in Orange that Mitterand, too, would be coming to the performance; if he had done so I think I would have ignored the demands of foreigners' etiquette and joined the faction applauding him.

The orchestra was yet another bad French orchestra. Not since the Conservatoire under Munch has any French orchestra been able to gain international recognition: even Britain, in that time, has had two such (though not both at once, and neither for very long), despite the fact that the conditions under which British musicians work make it almost impossible for any British orchestra to be really first-rate.

There was little in the way of production in the Orange *Don Carlos*; hardly surprising, as the stage is so wide and so shallow that performing there must be like acting on an unrolled bandage. Nor was there any serious attempt to provide settings; the huge, towering wall that forms the backdrop is so imposing, with its spotlit statue of Augustus in the middle of it, that it makes a designer's job both impossible and unnecessary.

There was, however, some fine singing. The acoustics of the theatre are perfect; I realised this before the performance began, when one of the metal posts holding the ropes that mark off different sections of the seating became loose, and a handyman was sent for. He knocked the post back into place, but the echo of every blow he struck on it – and he was fully two-thirds of the way up the shell of the building – instantly sprang back off the wall, a perfect replica of the metallic bang of the hammer. The result was that Montserrat Caballé, whose voice is always at its best when used at its most delicate, could project the gentlest and most flawlessly shaped phrase of the music with the softness that would render her inaudible in most ordinary opera-houses. What with that, and the thrilling chest-notes of Grace Bumbry,* the ladies had the best of it, though I remain convinced that of all the rival versions of *Don Carlos* the best is the shortest, and that if yet another should be discovered, an hour shorter still, I would transfer my allegiance to it immediately.

The tiny hotel (the town was very crowded) at which I was staying was run by a very jolly Corsican whom I instantly dubbed Mr Paunch. The paunch in question was massive, but what set this one off from the common run even of massive paunches was the fact that it was naked; the heat of the day, and indeed of the middle of the night (the opera did not finish until 1.30 a.m.), had impelled him to remove his shirt. He had not, however, removed his braces; because his trousers could not be fastened at the waist over the paunch, he wore them (I felt that he was in no danger of starting a fashion) *below* it, which meant that without the braces they would not stay up at all. Next morning, which was Bastille Day, I decided to leave early, and came down for breakfast. There was no one about but Mr Paunch, who had clearly been celebrating the fall of the Bastille from the moment the clock struck midnight, and when I asked him for breakfast he stared at me as though he had no idea of what I was saying, let alone why I was saying it. At length he managed to clear his head sufficiently to understand that there was a man in his restaurant who wanted some breakfast. He peered closely at me and asked whether I had stayed in the hotel the night before. I said I had, but he still wasn't convinced, so I dangled my room-key in front of his nose, whereupon he made me some coffee and went round the corner to

---

*I know that the classification of a singer's voice into head, throat and chest is absurdly old-fashioned and anatomically nonsensical into the bargain, but nobody has yet come up with a better way to distinguish between what certainly seem to the average listener to be distinct categories, nor has anybody convincingly denied that they do sound as though they are coming from the head, the throat and the chest respectively.

fetch some bread. The bread was just baked; I wondered whether, on a public holiday in Britain as complete as the Quatorze Juillet in France, a hotel-keeper would have been able to disappear for five minutes and come back bearing fresh and crusty bread straight from the baker's oven. I decided that he would not, paid my bill and went on my way.

I went on it past the *rue* Jean Hervé, Tragédien. I remember Hervé; he was in the Comédie Française the first time I ever saw the company, when I was still a schoolboy and they were on a post-Liberation visit to London; the Modern Languages department was taken up to town to see them at a matinée. It was *Ruy Blas* (when the French write bad plays they don't do it by halves), full of swashbuckling that was very impressive to a schoolboy. Because I knew what time we would be going back, I slipped off to pay a surprise visit to my home, but I got the timing wrong and missed the train, and there was an appalling row. On my way out of Orange I passed a street bearing a name that for some reason sounds perfectly natural in English but almost impossibly comic in French: Guillaume le Taciturne. I had already discovered, for the first time and to my great surprise, that this city was where the House of Orange got its name from; apparently Guillaume le Taciturne had extensive estates in this part of France, for all that he was a real Dutchman.

On the way to Sérignan, I crossed the Eygues, yet another of the candidates for the valley that Hannibal took when he turned east. Whether it was or was not his choice, it must have been near here that he had the encounter with the two brothers disputing a tribal throne, both of whom appealed to him to adjudicate on their claim. Hannibal, in the unlikely position of Solomon, decided in favour of Brancus, the elder (and the incumbent – his younger brother was trying to depose him). Brancus expressed his gratitude in the way that was of the greatest help to Hannibal; he provided the army with rations, supplies, new weapons and – most precious of all – boots. (My own boots were by now broken in; there is only one test for the comfort of any footwear – is the wearer conscious of them? Mine – now scuffed and grimy, to be sure – had long passed the test.)

Sérignan was as typical a village in Provence as there could be; the houses dribbled down the hill, and before them, like a welcome mat, was a lovely golden cornfield, in front of which was the inevitable avenue of planes, giving shade to the arriving traveller. On one of the trees was yet another poster advertising yet another of the tiny festivals with which Provence abounds during the summer, at Vaison-la-

Romaine. The list of artists and groups suggested that this one must be rather bigger than most of them, and I was about to feel that I would like to visit it for a day or two when my eye fell on the news that among the performers would be the Martha Graham Company. I at once stopped wishing myself there, despite the fact that even Martha Graham must be too old to perform now. Many years ago, I had unwisely gone to a performance by her company when she was still dancing; the mysteries of ballet are for me eternally insoluble, and invariably result in nothing but unbearable boredom – I have therefore not gone to the ballet more than once or twice in the past ten years or so. But the Martha Graham performance was much more than ten years ago, and many good judges of these matters assured me at the time that it was quite different from any ballet I had ever seen before (in which they were quite right) and that I would enjoy it. Never in my life, before or since, have I seen anything so grotesque and absurd as the lurching and posturing of which the evening consisted (especially Martha Graham's own performance), and eventually I was seized uncontrollably with an attack of giggles so powerful that I became helpless, and realised, without being able to do anything about it, that I was seriously disturbing the people all round me who were pretending (in a few cases I dare say not even pretending) to find this nonsense impressive, even enjoyable; after a time one of the theatre managers tiptoed down the aisle and invited me, very politely, to leave the theatre. I did so with alacrity and relief.

There were a few *tricolores* to be seen in Sérignan, notably of course outside the Mairie; strolling through the village I suddenly came upon, from behind, a bronze figure of a seated man, and I quailed at the thought of yet another statue of Frédéric Mistral. When I went round to the front of it, however, I discovered not only that it wasn't Mistral, but that it was a man far more interesting, with far greater achievements to his name – J. H. Fabre. The statue itself (presumably Fabre was born in Sérignan)* was a fine one; he was shown with magnifying glass in hand and a crisp straw hat on his head. Fabre was an amazing man, far ahead of his time; his work on insects was, I suppose, the first really scientific study of them, and yet he managed to mingle it with an extraordinary poetic fantasy-life that he created for them. His *Life of the Bee* influenced Maeterlinck, but Fabre can hardly be blamed for that, though

---

*Later: No, he wasn't; he was born in Sainte-Léone; what was his statue doing in Sérignan?

I am sure that if Maeterlinck had never been born the world would be a much better place, especially since we would not have Debussy's *Pelléas et Mélisande*. Fabre deserves his monument.

Just outside Rochegude, I saw a sight which, had I seen it immediately after leaving Châteauneuf-du-Pape, I would have put down to the effects of the wine; M. Gilbert Breton's work, however, was not a mirage or a dream. He makes a simple table-wine – there were beautifully tended vineyards on either side of the road – but his unique achievement lay in his topiary. Beside the road leading to his house there was a row of twelve fir trees, and he had cut them into the shape of giant wine bottles, fully twelve feet high; when I asked him why he had done this, he said he thought it would amuse passers-by. He told me that he had been working on the tree-bottles for fifteen years, but that he had been growing wine there all his life, and his father before him. I asked him whether wine-making was easy, and he said that on the contrary the work of the vines demanded 'Énormément beaucoup de travail'. I complimented him on his topiary, and suggested he should add a thirteenth, in the form of a corkscrew; he laughed, and said he had thought of adding a glass, at least, and might yet do so. I was quite sure that M. Breton had heard every possible joke on the subject of his liquid topiary, and was no longer put out, even if he ever had been, by the incredulity of the passers-by. Herostratus burned down the Temple of Diana at Ephesus solely to make sure that his name would go down to history; M. Breton has established his own more modest claim on the notice of posterity, and managed to do so quite harmlessly. Long may his kind prosper, for I sometimes think we shall know that civilisation has come to an end when the last eccentric dies.

At Tulette, I had been invited to join the Bastille Day festivities in the evening, preceded by a wonderfully French ceremony. Just outside the village there was a stretch of road which served as a bypass; all it bypassed was another stretch of road that was considered too full of bends for travellers' comfort; the new one was not much more than 200 yards long, but the argument over the construction of it had been going on for a decade, because Tulette lies right on the border of two *départements*, each of which thought the other should pay for the work. They might have put the problem, like Brancus and his brother, to Hannibal; in the end, the local MP had managed to sort it out in Paris, and lo! the road was about to be opened. First, however, it had to be closed, and the police arrived to stop the traffic from both directions. Two charm-

ing young children, a boy and a girl, dressed in their best finery, took up
position on either side of the point at which the new stretch of road
began, and a *tricolore* ribbon was unrolled across it, each of the children
holding one end. Then the Député made a speech and cut the ribbon,
distributing bits to the local officials who had been given the privilege
of accompanying him. I had slipped through the cordon and marched
abreast of them, attracting some odd sidelong glances as I did so, but the
Député, possibly thinking that I was an eccentric but important villager
whom it would be electorally unwise to offend, made the best of things
and snipped off a bit of the ribbon for me, too; it lies before me as I
write, looking rather like a medal-ribbon torn from some disgraced
warrior's uniform.

A delightful scene; but I had allowed myself to forget that politicians
are still politicians even on the other side of La Manche. A celebratory
drink had been arranged for the villagers and their nice new straight
road, and I thought I had better gatecrash that, too, if only to keep up
my role as the influential local madman. As we waited in the heat, with
the bottles and glasses spread out like the grapes of Tantalus on the
tables before us, the Député made another speech, and at once proved to
be one of those politicians who, once they begin to hear the sound of
their own voices, find it difficult to stop listening, and therefore to stop
talking. When he finally wound up, I licked my lips; hopes vanished at
once, however, when the Sous-Préfet launched into a speech that
managed, surely with the greatest difficulty, to be more boring, *and
longer*, than the MP's.

Now nightmare descended. The Mayor stepped forward to move a
vote of thanks; his speech was shorter than either of those we had
already endured (it could hardly have been longer), but when his thanks
had been seconded with a round of applause from the villagers, the
Député stepped forward again and, before my now wholly incredulous
eyes and ears, proceeded to make *another* speech, still longer and worse
than anything that had preceded it. Such oratory has the curious effect
of making the listeners' throats dry, rather than the speakers', and I fell
upon a drink, when opening time finally came round, like a man dying
in the desert.

I scarcely expect to be believed when I recount what happened a few
hours later. The holiday banquet had been laid on long tables in the
town square at Tulette; it seems that each of a group of seven villages in
the area takes it in turn to put on the dinner, and this year Tulette's duty
had come round again. We sat down, and the waiters stood with

bottles poised, whereupon M. le Député materialised and made another speech, *even longer and more boring* than any of those, including his own, that had been heard in the afternoon. He was followed again by the Sous-Préfet and the Mayor, both with speeches that rivalled his in length and quality; as my reason tottered, I discovered an important and astonishing difference between a British crowd listening to its politicians and a French one; had such a festive occasion in Britain been marred by a politician who wouldn't stop talking, he would have been silenced within not more than five minutes by the traditional method of the slow handclap, and if the whole sequence of speeches I had endured this day had been staged in Britain on some occasion of national rejoicing, somebody would have been lynched, or at the very least pelted, before nightfall. The terrible truth dawned on me only slowly; the French attitude to their politicians is clearly one of instinctive *respect*, rather than the surely better British response, which is one of amused but tolerant contempt.

Then things turned happy. Nobody near me at my table spoke any English, but my broken French proved adequate, and among the group was the village wag; normally the wag of any group is also the group bore, because he is conscious of his waggishness and feels obliged to play his role to the full, lest he should be deposed and a new group wag chosen in his place. The wag of Tulette, however ('This is my wife – that's my first wife over there, but I had to divorce her because she wouldn't stop talking'), was without self-consciousness, a genuinely funny man who (another, and vital, difference from the official variety of funny man) could also be serious.

In the circumstances, it was hardly surprising that the wine flowed with the talk, the food appeared in lavish quantities, and in Tulette on Bastille Day, whatever might be the case at the amphitheatre in Orange on the eve, efficiency reigned; as the first firework was lit, the lights in the square were cut, and the display – an impressive one for so small a place – was watched in total darkness broken only by the fireworks themselves, which were cheered, as good fireworks always are, by all present. Then the lights came on again, the band struck up, the dancing began, and gradually the Quatorze Juillet 1984 wound to a pleasant and memorable end.

12 *Sitting for my portrait in Avignon*   13 *The hotel that had seen better days*
14 *The Pont St Bénézet: Défense de danser*   15 *Château des Fines Roches: not what it seems*   16 *The men from Pagnol*   17 *Sleeping off M. Mousset's wine*

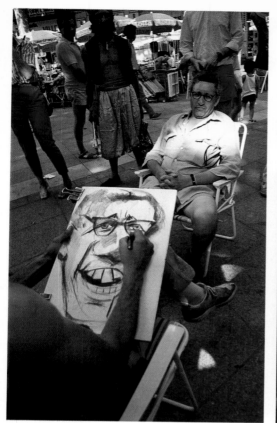

12

13

4

15

16

4

Half Way –
First Catch Your
Truffle

I MADE FOR St Paul-Trois-Châteaux, which does not have three castles, or two, or even one; it has none, and moreover never has had any. Enquiries as to how then it got its name met with no explanation other than that it may be a corruption, like those British pubs called the Goat and Compasses or Elephant and Castle which are supposed for no good reason to have been originally the God Encompasseth Us and the Infanta of Castile – alternatives which need considerably more explanation than the familiar and inexplicable ones.

The *mistral* had been blowing for three days and was almost over. The breeze from the tail-end was welcome; even more so was the effect of this extraordinary wind, which sweeps the sky like a giant broom, so that visibility seems to extend infinitely far, with only the horizon preventing a clear view of the people on Aldebaran and Alpha Centauri going about their daily business. If they can see us, what do they make of the next human achievement I came upon?

'Broiler-chicken' is a word that has passed into the language, with unambiguously pejorative associations; Raymond Postgate said of them that 'they taste of nothing but dry wood', an excellent description. As I left Suze-la-Rousse and came to a long metal shed full of squawking, I realised that I had never before set eyes on the broiler-house itself. It looked exactly as it does in photographs (the photographs are usually taken and circulated by groups opposed to broiler-chickens not because they taste horrible but because the chickens, they say, suffer unnecessarily); a long, low, ugly building, painted grey, with a row of small windows. I decided not to go and peer in at the windows, and certainly the hapless creatures could not look out; but the squawking pursued me far down the road. I quietened my conscience with the thought that I refused to eat them on culinary grounds; that would not satisfy the Chicken Liberation Movement, but I hoped it would satisfy the chickens.

The Café de Paris in St Paul-Trois-Châteaux lacked the luxury and elegance of its better-known counterpart in the capital, but it provided a perfect view of French café life. As I sat in the evening sunshine, I observed the rituals, as stylised and hieratic as anything from Ancient Egypt. First, the men, though in some instances they had met only an hour ago (indeed, one of them went through the ritual though he had risen from his table on some small errand round the corner and returned within ten minutes), invariably shook hands with all their acquaintances, if necessary travelling from table to table in order to do so. Next, between two acquaintances who were both women, or of opposite sex, three kisses were exchanged, and the formula was invariable; the one who arrived saluted the one already seated, kissing the right cheek, left cheek, right again. These rituals – both the shakehand (it is odd that they have adopted for it an English word, and moreover an English word that is not used in England) and the three kisses – were repeated when anyone left. The final ritual I saw next day, when I was having my breakfast; the custom of downing very large glasses of brandy at eight o'clock in the morning.

At Clansayes there was a colossal statue of the Virgin, standing on a rise and dominating the view from all directions. There had been another such at Rochegude. It was a singularly ugly statue, with a lot of the insipid blue that is to the Roman Catholic church what a certain sad, dark green is to British Rail, but it made me wonder yet again why the two streams of Christianity had argued so fiercely about the figure whom both, after all, acknowledged as the Mother of God. That Victorian phrase 'the cult of the Virgin' had always seemed to me an inexplicable sneer, and I had been obliged to put it on that back shelf of my mind where I had always kept my collection of similarly unintelligible differences of opinion, starting with a dusty box, unopened for years, labelled 'Transsubstantiation'.

The road to La Garde Adhémar presented a fine view of yet another French ritual: the practice of advertising a town along the road leading to it. La Garde Adhémar itself appeared to offer nothing of any consequence, but on the other side of the road there was a series of massive signboards proclaiming, with increasing frenzy, the delights of St Paul, now behind me. On one, the traveller was promised a *parc-auto*, ample *joie de vivre* and *ravitaillement facile*; the next offered St Paul's more sedate attractions: *sa cathédrale, ses vestiges, son site.* After that came a sign drawing attention to this braggart village's *piscine tempérée, snack, camping, tennis* and *terrasse ombragée*, and finally – though it was, of course, the *first* sign a traveller on the road from La Garde to St Paul would see – came the announcement: *St Paul-Trois-Châteaux, capitale du Tricastin, votre halte.* I knew nothing of the Tricastin (certainly not that St Paul-Trois-Châteaux was the capital of it) except that it produces truffles and quarrels with Périgord as to which variety is the finer. I had not tested the *piscine tempérée* or *terrasse ombragée* at St Paul, but I had looked into the Cathedral the night before and it was all that the traveller was led to expect; a vast vaulted roof, miles high, covering a surprisingly small nave – presumably able to accommodate easily the thirteenth-century congregation (and even more easily today's), and with a faint resemblance to that amazing basilica on Torcello, hard by Venice.

La Garde Adhémar proved to be a hill-village, perched right on the edge of the cliff above me, with only the church to prevent it falling off. (It gets its double-barrelled name from the two families – the La Gardes and the Adhémars – which successively provided its overlords.) The climb up was a stiff one, but well worth it, for La Garde turned out to be a perfectly preserved little spot, untouched by the world of today; it looked thousands of years old, and may well have been, and it was so unmodernised that I could find not a single shop, only tiny stone houses, arched doorways, oaken shutters, cobbled streets, and the sun beating down on everything. The views, particularly beneath the windswept sky, were spectacular and extensive, the fields laid out as if by a civil servant with a mile-long ruler, almost all of them surrounded by neat, wind-resisting hedges; corn and sunflowers abounded, but there were no vines – too high, perhaps.

On the outskirts of Donzère there was a depressing sight, the human equivalent of the broiler-house, a series of apartment-blocks, new but already shabby, looking as though someone had taken the worst of the London high-rises and laid them on their sides. Ghastly uncurtained windows stared blindly out, the ugly balconies had not a soul on them, before the doorways rubbish was strewn. It was no comfort to realise that the French had gone down the same mad road as we had, though it sharply reinforced the need for an answer to the unanswerable question of Britain's post-war building: why, as soon as the buildings had got high enough – say five or six storeys – for their nature to become apparent, did not the populace who were to live and work in them simply rise *en masse* and hang the architects and town planners responsible?

The hotel in Donzère turned out to be another of the sad places, slowly dying, which can never get enough slack in the rope of marginal profits to smarten themselves up. (Last night, at St Paul, the shower played the traditional role of the Sten gun – it poured water out backwards as soon as it was turned on.) In the *salon*, I found a 1959 Michelin and took it to bed with me, to send me to sleep half-drowned in nostalgia for the places I had known long ago, but which had disappeared over the years. Lapérouse, for one; there it was on the Quai des Augustins, with its three stars and its strange little rabbit-warren of tiny rooms. It has suffered a fate much sadder than simply disappearing; there is still a restaurant there with the same name, but it does not even warrant inclusion in the Guide today, let alone starred inclusion. And what became of the third star for the Poste at Avallon? It has had only two in all the years I have been going there, so it must have lost the third very soon after the 1959 edition. Of course, none of the *nouvelle cuisine* people were in the book then; Guérard was not yet at his place in Paris, which he ran for many years before he went to Eugénie-les-Bains and invented *cuisine minceur*. But at least the great Mère Brazier, in the hills above Lyon, was here, to remind me that I had not dreamed her establishment.

From Donzère, next day, it was only a short detour to the hydro-electric works on the Rhône and its canal. I have never understood anything about dams and locks, and standing in the middle of the canal here I still did not understand how it all worked. But a visitor to the 'défilé de Donzère' does not need to understand it to feel awe at the sight. There was a lock across the whole width of the water, with a gate the height of a three-storey house, a gigantic mill-race, and a vast complex of buildings, barriers and barrages that reminded me of Fritz Lang's *Metropolis*. I marvelled again at the extraordinary randomness of nature; if Britain thinks she has been hard done by in the matter of energy-producing rivers, what must Australia feel at the knowledge that she hardly has any rivers at all?

From the dam I went to meet M. Rimbaud, who was to hand me on to M. Escoffier, who had promised to take me truffle-hunting. M. Escoffier was a jovial fellow, and in turn he introduced me to his dog, Black. Black was a little mongrel, nine years old and going grizzled round the chops; he was very friendly, even licking my hand when I patted him. In the Tricastin, truffles are always hunted with dogs; it is only in Périgord that they use pigs. That much I knew, but I must have had a vision of a line of truffle-hunters advancing across country like a row of guns on the grouse-moors; on the contrary, M. Escoffier explained, it is a very solitary occupation, and he and Black did all the work by themselves.

Off we went; M. Escoffier held Black on a long lead, which he occasionally shook like a rein, and said only, again and again, 'Allez, Black, allez Black, allez, allez'. Thus encouraged or instructed, Black went; I thought it might be hours before the first truffle was sighted, and more hours before one was brought down, but to my amazement Black 'found' almost at once, scrabbling at the earth with his paws. M. Escoffier pushed him gently out of the way, stuck a fork in the ground at the spot, and out came a truffle nearly the size of my fist. Black got his reward with a little coloured biscuit – M. Escoffier explained that this was his favourite food – and on we went; it was only a few moments before Black was again scrabbling at the earth. So it went on, with truffle after truffle going into one side of M. Escoffier's pouch, and biscuit after biscuit coming out of the other side for Black. M. Escoffier explained that these were what were called 'summer truffles', inferior to the winter ones and without the full, rich scent (though to my nose the truffle-scent of these was almost overpowering).

Now it was my turn. I was sure that M. Escoffier must have had some trick for helping Black find the truffles, which I would never be able to reproduce, even if Black's own powers did not vanish at the realisation that he had a stranger at the other end of his lead instead of his master. I thought the best thing must be to do exactly as I had seen M. Escoffier do, so I gave the reins a shake and called out 'Allez, Black, allez Black, allez, allez, allez'; off went Black tugging gently at the line. Within a matter of seconds he was digging away; I pushed him aside very carefully and stuck in the fork. Up came a truffle, a small one; I was so amazed I stood there contemplating it, and Black darted in and gobbled it. I thought I had better give him his normal reward anyway, and fished out one of the biscuits, which he wolfed down after the truffle, and we set off again. Nor was my early success a flash in the pan; I, too, put a dozen or so truffles in the bag (though several more times Black was too quick for me and had scoffed the prize before I could get to it). M. Escoffier was wonderfully proud of Black, particularly since he had performed so well for the visitor; he said he would not take

10,000 francs for him. He also, in answer to my question, said that a good truffle-hound like Black would dig up, in the course of his lifetime, a ton of truffles; well, Black was certainly worth his weight in gold as well as truffles, for M. Escoffier said that the 'real' ones now fetch 1,200 francs a kilo at the local market. I felt that I could take to truffle-hunting without much difficulty, particularly if I had a dog like Black; it is by no means the back-breaking occupation I had thought it – the mild effort of bending for the truffle is more than offset by the pleasure of picking it up – and I like the idea of its being a trade plied only by one man and his dog. Perhaps, when I retire, I shall make M. Escoffier an offer for Black, and spend my days truffling as well as fishing. Better than writing for a living, anyhow, where there is no pleasure in eating one's words.

I had never spent a night in a monastery before, unless staying the weekend at Downside School counts. But earlier in the year I had visited Notre Dame d'Aiguebelle and been entertained by the briskly commercial air of the place, its shop selling wine and spirits, together with a liqueur distilled by the monks and honey made in their own hives, and in addition souvenirs, soap, lavender and even books on theology. The shop, as far as I could see on that occasion, was doing a roaring business; there was a constant inflow of customers and a constant outflow of the same customers now laden with packages. (I began to look round nervously for the horrible mad monk with the flapping sandals, so memorably portrayed in Rebecca West's *Black Lamb and Grey Falcon*, but closer inspection reassured me; jolly these monks might be, but they clearly took their vocation seriously.) I have always been fascinated by the idea of the monastic existence; I could never imagine myself part of it, but the man who literally shuts himself away from the world in order the more completely and purely to worship his God seems to me a man well worth studying. A cordial welcome was given to a request for me to visit the monastery and stay the night, and now here I was enquiring for the Guest Master. Instead, the Abbot appeared. Dom Bernard looked exactly as I had always supposed (on not much evidence, I confess) an Abbot should look; lean, wise, shrewd and holy. He greeted me and handed me over to Frère Paul, a monk of great sweetness and charm, with a secret joy in his heart. He said it was an honour to have me in the monastery; no doubt that was what he said to all the other guests as well as me, but if so, it was plain that he meant it to all the other guests, too. Frère Paul took me to the Guest Master, who looked me over quizzically; in the time it took him to blink he had clearly made up his mind that I was not monk-fodder, and in the time it took *me* to blink I realised that he was the monastery's card, with much the same combination of wit and seriousness as the Wag of Tulette. He gave Frère Paul a key, and Frère Paul took me to my cell.

Not quite a cell, at least not literally, but marvellously spartan. Bare, shabby walls, no covering on the boarded floor, a plain iron bedstead, on the wall at its head a fluorescent strip-light and a crucifix (an engaging marriage of two worlds). There was a washbasin with a cold tap only; beside it stood a jug, and Brother Paul led me down the corridor to a standpipe with hot water. In the corridor there were bare light-bulbs, of which some worked. It struck me at first as being not at all unlike the threadbare little hotels I had been staying in, and none the worse for that, but I realised that there was a different comparison nagging at me just outside memory, and after a time it abruptly came to me: it was exactly like being back at school. Boys' boarding-schools are always described by the cliché 'monastic institutions', and I realised for the first time that the cliché is perfectly apt; it has always been applied, of course, to the single-sex nature of the British Public School (though my own was to go fully co-educational by the end of 1984, and on a visit there a few months earlier I had reeled at the sight of electricians fixing sockets for hairdryers), but the description is at least as fitting for the simple plainness of the living quarters. We pamper ourselves too much – I do anyway; it had been no hardship to fetch my hot washing-water in a basin at school, and it was no hardship to fetch it in a jug in the monastery of Aiguebelle, but the difference in adjustment-time was the measure of the years between. Besides, soon after settling in I had been visited by the monastery kitten, who made it clear that he got too little play from the monks and looked to me to make up the deficiency; from then on, we went together on expeditions to seek hot water or the shower-room.

After supper, I went to the chapel for Compline, the last service of the day. It was chanted; I sometimes think I would exchange all the music I have ever heard or ever will hear for real plainsong heard amid walls of stone. There were full bows, almost prostrations, at the names of the Trinity, and at the end of the service, the monks filed out past the Abbot, each of them, in passing, being sprinkled by Dom Bernard with a few drops of holy water and given the blessing; when the last monk approached, he took the sprinkler from the Abbot and reversed the ritual. I was in bed by 9.30; apart from a brief hospitalisation some

twenty-five years ago, I could not remember an occasion on which I
had retired so early, but as I was going to Mattins at 5.45 (the monks
would have already had one service at 3.30) it seemed not such a bad
idea. Frère Paul had said that Mattins was sometimes late; as I dressed I
hummed the old round to myself, Frère Jacques, Frère Jacques,
dormez-vous, dormez-vous? Sonnent les Matines ...

Mattins was full of polyphony, an organ replacing yesterday's pitch-
pipe; the harmonies sounded coarse beside the memory of the plainsong's spare, clean beauty. Afterwards, I went to talk to the Abbot.
From Brother Paul I discovered that Dom Bernard had not been
imposed upon the monastery, but elected by the monks, who always
had a choice of electing an Abbot either for six years or for life; they had
to decide which it should be before going on to choose the incumbent.
A year before, after the death of the previous Abbot, they had decided
that the next one should rule for life, and had then chosen Dom
Bernard.

I asked the usual silly questions which those who preside over monastic orders are always asked, simply because there are no other questions.
Why the monastery? For the greater glory of God. Why the with-
drawal? To enable each monk to concentrate entirely on his spiritual
duty. Why the silence (Aiguebelle is Trappist)? To reduce all distraction
that hinders the inward search. Why the recent relaxations in the Rule?
A pause here before the answer, and the only answer that sounded not
entirely at ease: because the world has changed, and monasteries, too,
must take account of new conditions. (The rule of silence, I learned,
was no longer complete, but was still imposed on monks working in
the grounds, who were not allowed to speak to visitors, and in the
refectory; silence also reigned in the library – well, so it does in most
libraries. But no one could say that the monks led an easy life; with
breakfast at 4.15 *after* the first service of the day, they were hardly
pampered.) Was the supply of new monastic recruits diminishing? No
pause here, but a very surprising answer: it had fallen off in the 1960s,
but had picked up again. To think that that ill-starred decade had
washed against this rock!

Dom Bernard also told me that he has felt a vocation from the age of
nineteen, when he entered the Trappist Order; he had been Abbot
elsewhere for some years before he was chosen by the monks of
Aiguebelle, some of whom had been there for almost unimaginable
lengths of time; there was one tiny gnome among them, with a white
beard, seen stirring the saucepans in the refectory, and Dom Bernard

said that he was ninety-one, and had been at Aiguebelle for more than sixty years.

The Scriptorium, I felt, ought to have been the place where the monks illuminated manuscripts; in fact, it was the library, where they read. The silence was unbroken by even the smallest murmur, and I tiptoed about the shelves. There was a lot of modern theology, in many languages, as well as devotional and liturgical work of every kind. I plucked down a modern edition of the Vulgate, and a spider scuttled out from behind it – clearly nobody had been reading St Jerome's version for some time. Then I tried the Septuagint, and although there were no spiders there was plenty of dust, so presumably no one had been reading that lately either.

Brother Paul saw me off, repeating his assurance that it had been an honour. On the road in the bright sunshine, I found myself envying him. But precisely what was it that I was envying? The warmth of the cocoon that surrounded him? His certainty? The joy that peeped out again as we shook hands? His faith itself? To some extent, of course, all of these, but there was something else: his courage.

I thought back on my visit to the hydro-electric dam on the Rhône canal, with its gigantic installations, its millions of gallons of water, its production of energy to heat and light homes and factories, to drive machinery to make countless objects, including more machinery, its primary function – locks, gates, pipes, barrages, cables – to make life easier for millions of human beings. It had been only an hour or so from Aiguebelle, but an infinite distance, for all that.

Aiguebelle was founded in the twelfth century; the Rhône water-works three-quarters of the way through the twentieth. The world and the spirit, or the world visible and the world invisible; or the arena and St Trophime again. In a sense, the whole history of post-war Christianity has been the attempt to marry those two worlds, to make peace between the irresistible force and the immovable object. Had I imagined the tiny hesitation before Dom Bernard had answered my question about the relaxation of the Rule? I think not.

The truth is that I am unable to believe that when Christ said 'My Kingdom is not of this world' he meant that it was. Among the fifty monks of Notre Dame d'Aiguebelle, it was possible to see, misty but unmistakable, the point. The enclosing shell of a monastery becomes a symbol of what must be the ultimate truth not only of Christianity but of all religions: the Kingdom of Heaven is within. For the monks, within the walls; for the rest of us, within the human heart, which has room enough for all the walls there are. We all carry within our hearts a Notre Dame d'Aiguebelle, where we can find, though only if we seek diligently enough, the things of the spirit that alone make sense of the things of the world. Brother Paul seeks diligently enough; I don't. But the reason I don't can only be that I fear to find what I am seeking. That is why I said that what I envied about him was, in the end, his courage.

From the monastery to Montélimar; a greater contrast, perhaps, than there was between the hydro-electric works and the monastery. After all, the world, though in the end it will have to come to terms with the monastery, will still need the electricity. But who could possibly claim to *need* Montélimar? Dentists, certainly; who else? And surely even the dentists cannot need the suburbs of Montélimar, whatever they may think about the nougat-factories that give them such a handsome living.

Sooner or later, if some folk have their way, the whole of England will look like the centre of Birmingham. We like to think, romantically, that other countries, and particularly France, do not suffer from this creeping urbanisation, that there the countryside is inviolate and that nobody goes about looking for things to make uglier. It is not so; the disease has spread throughout Europe, and even if it here takes longer to infect the populace than it has in England, sooner or later the whole of La Belle France will end up looking like Clermont-Ferrand. Those little squares behind the high street still exist, but they are fewer than they were, and getting fewer all the time. Many houses still have their old, handsome shutters, but many more do not. Many French towns still practise the old religion of the pavement *apéritif*, but in many of them the traffic is too noisy for it to be accompanied by the equally traditional conversation about the iniquities of the government and the mystery of women. Montélimar, as it happens, had just such a little square, with just such shutters and just such peaceful contemplation of life. But it was hidden away behind the shops and the traffic, near the city centre yet remote from it, and there was no such square in the horrible suburbs. French suburbs, as a rule, are dull, and in general fairly ugly, but they do not exude hopelessness and dirt. The road into Montélimar exuded both in great measure, and what made it worse was that I was faced by the threat of nougat (a sweetmeat I have always detested) from the moment the buildings began to appear along the road. There were factories making it, shops selling it, hoardings advertising it, names incorporating it, signs portraying it; the very air reeked of its sickly scent, resounded with its two long vowels, tasted of its horrible, bland sweetness.

It is not generally known, though it should be, that the Mayor of Montélimar is weighed annually in nougat, in front of a Town Hall made entirely of nougat, that the local MP is obliged, if he wishes to keep his seat, to wear a hat made of nougat, that the restaurants serve nothing but nougat soup, nougat omelettes, nougat cutlets; I could hear all the townsfolk summoning their cats and dogs, all named Nougat; the bars became a blur before my eyes, all called the Café Nougat; eventually, my feet seemed strangely reluctant to leave the ground as I walked, and on looking down I was terrified by what I saw – pavements made of nougat.

In for a penny . . . I visited a nougat factory, and was shown round by the owner. It was, I suppose, everything I expected a nougat factory to be: clean, obviously hygienic, full of Heath Robinson machinery for wrapping and boxing the stuff. There was one machine which emitted small blocks of nougat, wrapping each one neatly in cellophane as it did so; the feeding of the machine with the blocks, however, was done by hand, and a girl stood beside it putting blocks from a huge mound into slots on a disc, each block being then mechanically whisked from its hold and carried up to the wrapping arms. I watched her for quite a long time, and became convinced that the operator of this machine would have to be replaced every few months, as one by one the holders of the position were taken away to the lunatic asylum. Eventually, I asked the girl doing it whether she did not get bored, and she said that she did not, which I took as evidence that she was ready to be removed and replaced by a new, sane one.

The vats in which the ingredients were mixed and cooked were all automated, apart from the process of pouring in the correct amounts of glucose, honey and almonds, all of which stood in vast quantities on tables. There was a massive tray of almonds waiting to go into the mixer, and I picked up a couple and ate them, whereupon the full horror of nougat, which I thought I had long since plumbed to its depths, now became apparent to me for the first time. The almonds were *perfectly* fresh, presumably only just gathered and shelled; no almond I had ever eaten could compare, even remotely, with the succulence, crispness and full flavour of these. I simply did not know, and realised I never had known, what almonds really tasted like. And this incomparable living fruit was going to have that taste crushed out of it, glucosed out of it, mixed out of it, boiled, cooled, flattened, sliced, wrapped and boxed out of it. I thought I was going to burst into tears, and staved them off by taking an entire handful of the kernels and nibbling them, one by one, for the rest of my tour of the factory.

The history of the stuff made appalling reading. The name came from an ancient cake or sweetmeat called Nux Gatum, or Nougo, said to have been introduced by the Greeks when they colonised Marseille. (There is a ghastly version which makes it a corruption of 'Tante Manon, tu nous gâtes'.) The almond-tree arrived in France in the seventeenth century, and nougat was promptly invented; its finest hour was in 1701, when three princes of the blood royal were making a progress through France. When they got to Montélimar the citizens marked the honour the princes were doing the town by presenting them with a hundredweight of the stuff.

The last thing I learned from the nougat-maker was that Montélimar made some 30,000 tons of it annually. I could not bring myself to tell this charming man that that was the worst news I had heard for many years, and I managed to look pleased, as well as grateful, as I carried away the box of nougat with which he had presented me as I left. Half a mile later, looking round carefully to make sure that I was not observed, I threw it into a litter-basket.

At some point, Hannibal had to turn east and prepare for the climb. Exactly where he did it is one of the cruxes of the story, and has been a matter of conjecture for two thousand years. I had decided earlier on that from all the candidates he had picked the valley of the Drôme. It was broad; it went for a considerable distance directly towards his goal, it ascended gradually, and it brought him out with a reasonable choice of passes for the final stages of the climb. All those considerations weighed with me, too, and in addition I knew that it went through some of the most beautiful and varied countryside in France. It also seemed to make sense for him to cut off the corner rather than follow the Rhône all the way to Loriol and turn sharp right. At Montélimar, then, I decided I would follow the wide valley through which flow two rivers, the Vermenon and the Roubion. But before I did so, I knew that I had to make a detour, and that the detour was really more of a pilgrimage.

Jacques Pic is the most modest and self-effacing of the French three-star chefs ('Just because we have a little success', he says, 'we must not swell up like frogs'), but he has nothing at all to be modest about. Valence is not much of a town, and it would have few visitors other than those on business if it were not for Pic. He inherited the restaurant from his father, after a long period of wondering whether he wanted to be a chef at all. André, Pic *père*, had built the restaurant up, star by star, to the rarefied, and demanding, heights of three. Too demanding; his health broke down, and he lost one star, then a second. At that point, Jacques stilled all his doubts and took over. The downward trend was halted, then reversed; he got the second star back, then the third. He is in no danger of losing it, and his health is excellent.

I had always believed, before I met it, that his Menu Rabelais was so called because it is gargantuan, and those who ate it had to be carried from the table by four strong men. Then I did eat it, and realised that, although it consisted of eight courses, it was not rabelaisian in the accepted sense of the word at all. So why the name? M. Pic explained; Rabelais was a student at Valence (where, I later discovered, he had had an affair with his tutor's daughter), and the menu was named in his honour. (Napoleon was also a student at Valence, but he cared nothing for what he ate and drank.)

In the lobby a weird animal, either a dog the size of a bear or a bear that looked like a dog, took up most of the floor; its name was Giankin, and it was said to be harmless. Once past Cerberus, I looked round the restaurant; handsome but not ostentatious, let alone over-decorated, its background announced that serious things were done here. And indeed they were.

I started with a bottle of Pic's own *marque* of champagne; his friend Peynet, who draws those innocent and touching pairs of lovers, had designed the label, which of course shows his lovers in a bower. I pored long and carefully over all the menus and the *carte*; it was only curiosity, for I knew I was going to take the Menu Rabelais.

It began with a little melon and Parma ham, just to start the juices flowing. There followed fillets of red mullet accompanied by quail's eggs stuffed with caviar. After that there was an *escalope de fois de canard* in a lemon sauce, with razor-cut shreds of lemon sprinkled on it; the taste and delicacy of the dish suggested that Pic should be burned at the stake for sorcery. The same was true of the next course, tiny, curled-up *écrevisses* in a pastry boat, lavishly decorated with truffles.

At this point came the 'trou Normand', in Pic's case a lemon sorbet drenched in *marc de l'Hermitage*, which with perfect timing did its job of anaesthetising the palate for a few minutes until it came back to life at exactly the moment that the next dish arrived. This was a mixture of poached *loup de mer* and salmon, in a creamy vegetable sauce, and arranged in tiny fragments so that the white of the sea-bass contrasted with the pink of the salmon; it might have been knitted on to the plate, so carefully and delicately had it been arranged. As for the sauce, Van Gogh would have given his other ear to paint it, so beautifully coloured was it, with the flecks of the various vegetables dotting the yellowish base. After that came the pigeon, in wine. I do not normally care for pigeon; I find it too strong, but this one happily lacked the too-gamy taste, and the meat fell away like the most delicate chicken.

The cheeseboard was in perfect condition, of course, and I took two of the local *chèvres*; a big, creamy one, slightly fiery on the palate, and a few of what they call 'trouser-buttons' – tiny, very hard pellets, with a straw through them, that go down in one bite each.

A huge array of desserts arrived, their number and beauty exceeded only by that amazing cornucopia provided at Chapel. First, however, the waiter produced a *soufflé glacé à l'orange*; this, he said, in a delight-fully chosen word, was 'obligatoire'. I did not refuse my obligations, and was rewarded by one of the most subtle and memorable tastes I have ever experienced. Then from the *choix de desserts* I chose some raspberries and *fraises des bois*, with a peach sorbet. After that the waiter came back with the pastries on a separate trolley; I shook my head, and I thought he was going to burst into tears. I shook it again and he cried 'I've been here for twelve years, and I've never had anyone refuse them yet', so I gave in and had the chocolate *gâteau*, and then he said 'What about the *millefeuille* as well?', but this time I stood firm, so he took his revenge by presenting a plate of the most irresistible *friandises*.

I had put myself in the hands of the *sommelier* after the champagne; he recommended a white Hermitage, which was a wonderfully flowery one, like the biggest Sancerre but with the refinement Sancerre doesn't have, and a red Hermitage to follow, which I had to admit would win hands down over all the Châteauneuf-du-Pape I had ever had, and a great deal of the best Burgundy, too. After all that, I went out into the garden and lay down on a lovely, soft, pink *chaise-longue* and had a nice, long, dreamless sleep, then woke up, drank a litre of Badoit and felt that life was really very agreeable. Then I found Pic himself at my side, asking if all had been well, and I assured him that all had indeed been well, very well. 'J'ai mangé des miracles', I said, and he actually blushed. 'And you do it every day!' He shrugged and smiled; 'C'est mon métier'.

Next day, *Figaro* greeted me with the news that Mitterand had sacked his Prime Minister, Mauroy, and appointed Fabius instead. I had never heard of Fabius, but I took the news as a good omen, because it was

Fabius Maximus, dubbed 'Cunctator' because of his use of delaying tactics, never risking a pitched battle, who finally wore Hannibal down. That is where the Fabian Society got its name, and a Hannibalic reference, however oblique, was encouraging.

With these thoughts, I set off for a village with the curious name of Le Poët Laval. I had an image of a middle-aged man in a rather old-fashioned three-piece suit, walking with an ebony stick, pince-nez dangling from a cord in his buttonhole ... meet my friend the poet Laval. Not *the* poet Laval? A self-deprecating shrug. Ah, Monsieur Laval, how I admire your sonnets. Thank you, thank you, they are nothing ...

The sonnets could wait; I had heard a rumour that necessitated another detour.

I was always on the lookout for elephants. I knew that Hannibal-hunters had always been searching for elephantine traces; why should not I find an entire skeleton, a tusk or two, a picture of one scratched on a rock, together with an inscription, by the official war-artist to the Carthaginian forces? Well, one reason why not was that I am too unobservant; I would have to trip over the tell-tale bones to have any chance of noticing them. Another was the insistence of Polybius that Hannibal lost no elephants on the march, and that they began to die, from the cold and the privations they had endured, only when the army was down on the Italian plains. The remains at Maillane seemed to contradict Polybius, and if Hannibal lost one elephant, why not two?

Of course, I realised that by now any evidence that Hannibal passed this way would be deeply buried, recoverable only by an archaeological dig, but that could not stop me dreaming; a sudden landslip, a rock avalanche, a collapse of a stretch of river-bed, and lo! the evidence, buried for twenty-two centuries, would lie before me (provided, of course, that I had not been swept away in the landslip, buried under the avalanche or drowned in the river). That odd-looking mound; suppose I poked it with my walking-stick? That precariously-balanced boulder; could I give it a shove hard enough to roll it over? That very curious depression in the earth beside my path; surely someone hereabouts could lend me a spade?

My yearning unassuaged, and the rumour I had heard tempting me, I walked into Cléon d'Andran, and saw *three* elephants. True, they were made of stone and adorned the village fountain; moreover, they were very plainly of late twentieth-century make. All the same, the trio stood in the fountain, their tails together, symmetrically placed (they made a figure like the Mercedes trade-mark) and their trunks, from which the water poured, raised. No matter that the villagers, asked whether their fountain commemorated a legend that Hannibal had stopped here, made it clear that they had never heard of him; no matter that here (as, indeed, along the whole of the route) there was not so much as a Café Éléphant, a Bar Hannibal, a Hôtel de Carthage; no matter that as I lingered by the fountain I received suspicious looks from those who plainly believed I had come to steal the goldfish; the symbolism of my *trouvaille* raised my spirits to Alpine heights, and I marched on as confidently as if I had dug up Hannibal's diary. As Michelin says: 'Mérite le détour', nay, 'Vaut le voyage'. And I was back on the road towards Le Poët Laval.

The distance before me was longer than my average, but it was a fine day, and I was in no hurry. There came to mind Hazlitt's essay *The Fight* (which I think is the finest piece of descriptive reporting any journalist has ever written); he passed the night before the bare-knuckle encounter at an inn, and since there were no beds to be had by the time he arrived, he stayed up all night talking, and next morning wrote casually 'Nothing but a nine miles march to Hungerford'. It had not occurred to him that to walk nine miles first thing in the morning was either an odd thing to do, or a particularly laborious one. But the reason he thought nothing of the walk was that he could not envisage any other way of getting there, because there *was* no other way, either for him or for the other spectators except the rich men in their carriages. A stage-coach had taken him as far as Brentford, and his legs would take him the rest of the way. The reason we grumble today at having to walk anywhere is not, I believe, that we are lazy; it is a matter of expectation. Trains, buses, taxis, and above all private cars, have made it natural, almost a matter of instinct, to go everywhere on wheels. The lack of such wheels for Hazlitt made it natural and a matter of instinct to go on foot.

As if in reply to these thoughts, there suddenly appeared a signboard beside the road, advertising 'Vente de chevaux', 'Équitation', 'Promenade à cheval' and 'Leçons de mise en selle'. It did not take much debate for me to decide that I would not buy any horses, go riding or walking on any horses, take lessons on how to put myself in the saddle of any horses. I have never sat on a horse, and the horses have responded, noble beasts that they are, by never sitting on me. And that, I long ago decided, was how it would be for the rest of my life. As for the *mise en selle*, the only saddle I am interested in is a saddle of lamb, and perhaps there would be one on the menu at Le Poët Laval. And here was a signpost for a village called Dieulefit, which presumably means 'God did it', though exactly what God did hereabouts is not explained.

The road to Laval the Poet (he had become Welsh somewhere along the route) wound through some of the most beautiful scenery so far; some of the big meadows were four-fifths corn and one-fifth lavender, and the result looked like a giant flag – a series of giant flags, as the proportions of golden corn and purple lavender varied; sometimes the lavender strip was at the side, sometimes at the top or bottom, sometimes in the middle, sandwiched between two sides of the corn. Perhaps this was what God did to be commemorated in the village name.

Above the fields there were thickly wooded hillsides, the green being just that English shade which makes Americans gasp. Van Gogh and Constable could have teamed up here; Van Gogh would have done the fields and Constable the woods and the cows. I don't know who would have been best for the trout farm I passed (a sight I was more familiar with from Germany than France), but the fish looked plump and succulent, and I was tempted to knock on the door of the retail department and buy one for my lunch. The other business enterprise I kept coming upon in these parts was the Atelier Poterie; there were so many that I could not imagine them being very profitable. One never knows, though; I remembered Le Cyclope, the place on the shores of Lake Annecy which sold what I think must have a fair claim on the title of the most hideous human artefacts ever created. Every single dish and bowl, vase and figurine, was of a stupendous ugliness, and I could never imagine how even a totally blind tourist (Le Cyclope indeed) could have brought himself to buy any; yet it was a vast establishment and seemed to stretch further along the bank every time I returned, so it must presumably have done good business.

To my urban eye, the corn had long looked ready for reaping, and at last the farmers were heeding my advice; I was passing the first cut fields, the stubble looking forlorn and naked after the crammed wheat I had seen earlier. Ahead, I could see Le Poët Laval, apparently wound round a hill, with the modern village nestling at the foot; I presumed that my hotel, Les Hospitaliers, would be in the old part, and so it proved. The old village was far more self-conscious than La Garde Adhémar; it even had a museum, and enamel plates directing the visitor to the various sights he should see; clearly, they were on the lookout for tourists, or at least used to them, and familiar with their needs.

Certainly they were familiar with my needs at Les Hospitaliers; the place obviously deserved its red type in the *Guide Michelin*, and after dinner I felt also that it deserved its food star. It was privately owned; Monsieur was the *sommelier*, Madame ran the front-of-house. Dinner was on the terrace, with views of the hills changing colour as the sun went down, then throwing their own shadows on their neighbours. A charming gesture from Madame; towards the end of dinner it began to be a little chilly *al fresco*, and she toured the tables offering the ladies the choice of a stole from the heap of vividly coloured ones she had over her arm.

The road began to climb at last; it was not to cease doing so, except in short stretches, until I was across the final pass and the frontier. As I raised my eyes to the great stone curtain of the Alps that hung in the sky before me, I realised it was just as well for me that Hannibal went from the Mediterranean to Italy rather than the other way round. By the time the road became really difficult, I reflected, I would be in the best possible shape to face it; as it was, I already felt fit, and my damaged back, which had caused me to call off this trip two years before, only a few days before I was due to set out, might never have come apart at all; indeed, even as that thought crossed my mind, it was followed by an even more encouraging one, which was that for several days now I had not once thought of my back at all, let alone with foreboding.

The foreboding now was for the long march over the Alps. I comforted myself with Livy's description of the scene that met Hannibal's eyes only a little further along this road; surely, it couldn't be as bad as that for me:

> The terrible vision now met their eyes; the towering crags, the snow-covered peaks soaring to the skies, the little huts hanging from the rocks, cattle and other beasts all drawn and parched from the cold, the tribesmen covered in matted hair, all nature, whether animal or mineral, frozen and rigid – all this, and in addition sights so dreadful that words cannot convey their horror, renewed and sharpened their fear.

When Hilaire Belloc started on the journey that resulted in *The Path to Rome*, he swore that he 'would take advantage of no wheeled thing'. He broke his vow, sensible fellow, almost immediately; I took care not to make any such rash promise to the capricious gods, though I did resolve not to hitch-hike, and kept my vow. But the detour I had just made by taking advantage of a wheeled thing could not have been encompassed

except by adding a good many days on to my timetable; and it was
something I did not want to miss.

By the standards of his time, indeed by the standards of any time,
Hannibal was an exceptionally magnanimous general; of vengeance in
conquest he was almost entirely free. *Nous avons changé tout cela.* Forty
years ago, to the day, there was a pitched battle in the Vercors between
the French Resistance and the SS. Such encounters were normally
avoided by the *maquis*, as they could never hope to match either the
numbers or the firepower of the German occupying forces, but here, at
a little village called Vassieux, there was a centre of the Resistance, and a
secret hospital, for wounded *maquisards*, in a nearby cave. On the arrival
of the SS troops, mostly in gliders, the men of the *maquis* thought at first
that they were Americans; D-day was only a few weeks' old. When
they discovered their mistake, they had no option but to stand and
fight. They were wiped out, and the SS took a bloody revenge by
massacring almost the entire population of the village and the occupants
of the cave hospital as well; then they razed the buildings, leaving only
the church standing. The atrocity at Vassieux was less widely known
than the one at Oradour, perhaps because the particularly gruesome
method of the murders at the latter had fixed it indelibly in the world's
consciousness; but it had never been forgotten at the village, and the
area's main cemetery for the Resistance was established just outside
Vassieux, together with a tiny Chapel of Remembrance, in which
visitors can see a twenty-minute slide show, with a recorded commen-
tary, that tells the story of what happened on July 22nd 1944.

Here it is necessary to pause, and to think about the French Resistance
in the days of Occupation. All nations need their myths, and none more
than the defeated. It has long been a truism to say that Britain's greatest
disaster of arms in the Second World War – the rout of the British
Expeditionary Force in 1940 – was turned into, and in British history
remains, an epic triumph, the magic wand that turned night into day
being the eternally evocative name of Dunkirk.

So it was with the French Resistance. The men and women of it were
brave beyond the imagination of most of us; they faced more than death
in battle – hideous torture and a prolonged dying in a concentration
camp. 'La nécropole de la Résistance' at Vassieux holds the bodies of
heroes and heroines, without any doubt at all. Only, there weren't very
many of them. The belief – it was the French equivalent of Dunkirk –
that virtually the whole of France, with the exception of a handful of
collaborators, was united in resistance to the hated occupier, and fought

him at every turn, was a giant myth. Most of France collaborated passively, and a very large number actively; it was those who fought the occupying troops who were the handful.

He jests at scars that never felt a wound; only a hero can call others to be heroic. It was de Gaulle, who *was* a hero, who recognised that if France were to regain her self-respect and her strength she must be given such a myth as the Resistance provided; he offered full encouragement to those who recognised the need to demonstrate that the Resistance involved the whole of the nation. It was many years later, with films like *Le Chagrin et le Pitié*, that France began to come to terms with the truth about the Occupation; she could not have faced it earlier. And it was de Gaulle's genius that he not only gave her a myth to sustain her, but managed in doing so to turn his countrymen away from the other, fatal myth that until then they had clung to – the myth of betrayal by King Leopold or the British, which they needed to believe because they could not bear the pain of realising that they had collapsed in the first real encounter of the war.

The Germans, of course, had a far greater trauma to heal. Their entire country was in ruins, the hideous shame of Nazism hung over them like a stinking cloud, and a third of the survivors, on the other side of the Elbe, were being incorporated into another totalitarian world even as they emerged from the one they had inhabited for twelve years.

Adenauer's genius was even greater than de Gaulle's. He could offer the Germans only blood, toil, tears and sweat, without even the consolation of a myth parallel to de Gaulle's Resistance one. He told them that they had nothing but their own hands with which to dig themselves out of the rubble, nothing but their own purged resolution with which to make Germany great again. And it was no accident that he put in the forefront of his policy a true reconciliation with France, just as it was no accident that de Gaulle at once saw that such a movement was the greatest, perhaps the only, hope for Western Europe. Apart from Churchill, those were unquestionably the greatest European statesmen of the post-war world, and they laid the foundations of Europe's future.

Here at Vassieux it was easy to see how the myth took hold; on the wall of the Chapel of Remembrance there was a simple but telling inscription, carved in the stone: 'Ils ne veulent pas nos regrets. Ils veulent survivre par notre courage et notre foi.'

When I arrived for the ceremony commemorating the battle and the massacre, an almost Orange-like state of administrative chaos reigned, and the chances of the timetable being adhered to seemed extraordinarily remote. Round the perimeter of the cemetery stood a ring of veterans carrying flags; along the road from the village to the scene of the commemoration there were detachments of troops, including the Spahis with an indefinable but unmistakable air of knowing their position as a *corps d'élite*. In the temporary stands there sat more veterans (and, I dare say, a good few collaborators), officers of all the services, men from the Ministry, foreign diplomats, mayors and other local worthies, and members of the families of those who died, including the one villager, then a young girl, who escaped the slaughter. There was also a band, the brass section of which would not have got far in auditions for the Chicago Symphony Orchestra.

The hills around were sharp against the cloudless sky; the village (very badly restored, in an exceptionally ugly style) is very high, and my wheels had had a spectacular climb to get there. (There was no road at all at the time of the battle, only a track.) A huge contingent of police formed a cordon round the crowd; others were dotted about in clumps at strategic points; with the number of VIPs already present, and the imminent arrival of the Minister of Defence by helicopter, no chances were being taken.

The buzzing of a giant hornet could be heard approaching; the huge helicopter landed, only a few seconds behind schedule, and the Minister emerged, accompanied by the Speaker of the Chambre des Députés. A brisk review of the troops ensued, and then the speeches began. Three men, one of them a *maquis* veteran, made a curious kind of joint speech, passing the theme back and forth; it was almost like a play, and they must have rehearsed it carefully. When they finished, it was the Mayor's turn, and after him the Minister, who was surprisingly concise. In the stands, an elderly woman in black wept quietly; among the crowd, another was being led gently away; a third, a little later, was carried by on a stretcher.

The Minister, accompanied by a guard of honour, disappeared into the Chapel of Remembrance to relight, symbolically, the perpetual flame; when he emerged, the veterans raised their standards and a double line of *tricolores* filed out of the cemetery gate. As I was talking into my tape-recorder, one of the officers asked me whether I had been recording the speeches; I didn't want to disillusion him, so I said 'Oui', and he nodded with great satisfaction at the thought that this foreign journalist should have recorded the immortal words of the Minister of Defence of France.

It was almost over; the band struck up the 'Song of the Resistance', which turned out to be a rather dirgelike melody, made more so by the fact that the male-voice choir started off in far too low a key, so that within a couple of verses the tenors had given up and only the basses were surviving. But there was one final, stunning moment; as the song ended, seven fighters roared overhead, only a few hundred feet above the ground, in perfect line abreast, and as they passed over the scene they left behind them seven columns of smoke, a central white stripe with three blue on its left and three red on its right.

The Minister returned to his hornet, which took off at once; I waited until the crowd had gone, and entered the Chapel of Remembrance. Sitting in the twilight there, I reflected that there had been an irony in the day much more telling and important than the irony of the Resistance myth. The massacre of Vassieux took place on July 22nd 1944; only two days earlier, another group of men and women, their very existence unsuspected by the heroes who fought and fell here, had joined hands with their French comrades from the other side of the Rhine, in an effort to end not only Nazi atrocities but the Nazi regime itself, and the war as well. The heroes of the German Resistance, who on July 20th placed the bomb beneath Hitler's table, died deaths more horrible even than those suffered by their French counterparts, but they had made the same point: *voilà l'ennemi*. Evil must be resisted, and the nationality of the resisters is unimportant. Killing, in battle or in such action as the Resistance movements undertook, is, like all killing, horrible, degrading, corrosive and wrong. But there are some things *more* horrible, degrading, corrosive and wrong than the taking of human life, and the eternal night of the great tyrannies of ideology is among them. If the Nazis had won the war, Europe would have fallen into a new Dark Age from which she might never have emerged; the French who fought the SS on this beautiful hillside were doing what Claus von Stauffenberg and his comrades were doing in Hitler's bunker, and both were engaged in the same work as the Allied armies — trying to ensure that that darkness did not fall. It is not quite impossible that the world will once again have to face the question: is there not something more terrible than war? The heroes of the French Resistance, and those of the German Resistance, answered that question in the words of the inscription on the wall of the Vassieux Chapel of Remembrance: they do not want our sympathy; they want to live on through our courage and our faith. Or, as the English verse which is the exact equivalent of those words puts it: if you break faith with us who die, we shall not sleep though poppies grow in Flanders field.

George Orwell, who would have been made uneasy by the expression of such sentiments in such fine words, put it all in his own plainer, yet no less telling style, when he said 'If a man proposes to drop a bomb on your mother, the only way to stop him is to go and drop two bombs on *his* mother.' The terrible truth is that evil, when it is in arms, can be defeated only by arming good. Can we fight fire with fire, cast out Satan with Beelzebub? Alas, yes.

I forgot to mention that when the troops marched off at the end of the Vassieux commemoration ceremony they were applauded, long and warmly, by the crowd; and by none longer or more warmly than the elderly women in black.

5

The Foothills –
Goat and Compasses

HERE I TOOK a rest; which, incidentally, Hannibal did not. He could not afford to; winter was closing in on the Alps, there would be snow soon and the passes would be blocked, perhaps impenetrably. Time enough to rest when they were down on the lush green plains of Italy; first they had to get there. And despite his stirring words to his troops, urging them to defy the Alps and conquer them, he knew, and the army must by now have begun to suspect, that if there was no way over the mountains because of the snow, they would all perish, trapped in a land that would not sustain life. Hannibal certainly knew the history of the events in Carthage that had followed the first Punic War – none better, for it was Hannibal's own father, Hamilcar, who at that time had led the Carthaginian army against the revolt of the city's unpaid mercenaries in alliance with her slaves, and had won the savage battle by exterminating the entire force arrayed against Carthage, down to the last man. What Hannibal was remembering now was not just that most of his own troops were mercenaries, but, more pressingly, that the final detachment of Carthage's enemies had died of starvation trapped in a mountain defile. And here was the son of the man who had led those victims into the trap, leading his own men into a gamble from which he could no longer withdraw even if he had wanted to, a gamble which might well end with a hideous death by starvation in another mountain defile. With as little rest as he dared to give his men, he pressed on towards his rendezvous with winter.

My own timetable was less inflexible. Winter was months away, and the likelihood was that I would arrive at my chosen pass, 9000 feet high,

19

20

21

24

29

26

in the middle of blazing August; nor would all be lost even if I didn't. Hannibal's army would rapidly have been reduced to eating marmots and other Alpine fauna, then their own pack-animals, then what roots and berries they could garner, and finally their own dead; for me, however, things would not be quite so grim even if every pass was closed. So far, on this journey, I had never been more than a few kilometres from a *steak et frites*, and even when I gazed at Italy with a wild surmise, the same would continue to be true. Of all the leaps of the imagination that a modern man must make when he tries to compare himself with the ancients, the most difficult, I have always found, is to feel the absence for them of the simplest and most rudimentary elements of our own civilisation. It is difficult enough to hold in view the thought that Hannibal's army had no maps and no roads; it is much more difficult still to understand the implications of the fact that along their route there were no shops, no wholesalers or factors, no system of food distribution or transport. On top of that, his version of the eternal problem of lengthening supply-lines faced by an army on the march was the most extreme possible; he had *no* supply-lines, for to keep his army provisioned from home, Carthage would have had to send a second army at least as great as the first, and another to supply that one, and then another to ...

So I paused, staying *chez* Mme Hoffet in a large house at Mirabel, between Crest and Saillans, and took stock.

We all, in order to stay alive in more than the merely literal sense, devise challenges to our powers; as we grow older, the need for such challenges grows stronger. One of the most powerful impulses in the human psyche, surprisingly little examined in any scientific manner, is the need to stave off the knowledge that we grow older, that eventually we grow too old, and die. To convince themselves that this is not true, many men have their teeth capped and many women have their faces lifted. These are very obvious methods of trying to deny the undeniable; there are more sophisticated versions available. One of them, largely confined to men, is the attempt to achieve success in physical activities usually engaged in only by the young, particularly the young whom he remembers best. For a man to emulate the son of the couple next door is satisfying, but for him to emulate his own youthful self is much more so.

Though I was not trying to make progress, I thought it best to walk my usual daily ration; the stiffness in my legs during the first few days of the

24 Jacques Pic: genius loci   25 Vassieux: old men remember   26 Elephants at last

expedition, as muscles not really tested in use for many years protested at being woken from their long hibernation, had convinced me that if I slackened off I would have to start again from the beginning. I was on the northern side of the Drôme; the golden cornfields were now falling fast to the sickle, or more precisely to the combine harvester, and the stubble looked as though it would itch the field beneath it to scratching fury. The river, which I could glimpse every now and again through the bushes, seemed low enough to wade across, in places to walk dryshod with only a hop or two to clear a puddle; there was drought all round this area, as indeed there was in most of Western Europe, and although there had been an occasional growl of thunder in the past few days, not a drop of rain had fallen.

Coming in to Blacons, I saw a very stern sign, headed 'Village propre' in letters bigger than the name of the village itself. It went on to advise the traveller that he could park there, and enjoy the various delights on offer, provided he disposed tidily of his rubbish, and it ended with the memorable slogan, 'La propreté de la nature est l'affaire de tous; emportez vos déchets après une pique-nique.' Once again, I was reminded of those two extraordinary and touching facts about Glyndebourne: the gardens and grounds, by deliberate policy, have no litter-baskets, and the visitors respond by invariably obeying the request to take their litter away with them, for in more than thirty years of Glyndebourne-going, I have never seen a scrap of rubbish anywhere. It is a lost cause, of course; though Glyndebourne and Blacons may hold out longer than most places, the world will eventually be covered by a layer of rubbish so deep that archaeologists centuries later may never get far enough down to discover what the rubbish had covered. Nor is the rising tide to be explained solely in terms of people's increasing indifference to their surroundings or to the feelings of others; we are simply producing more rubbish than we can get rid of. Palliatives have been, or are being, developed; the 'biodegradable' plastic bottle, for instance, which, when discarded, will eventually crumble away and return to the earth (except that it never came from the earth in the first place); but such devices will only hold up the tide for a moment, not reverse it, and the evidence, Blacons or no Blacons, was all around me as I walked. Gloomy thought, dispelled by the simultaneous realisation that I wanted some breakfast and that I was passing a café that might serve me some; and so it did. Did I want *petits-pains* or *croissants*? 'Tous les deux, madame.' 'Parfait.' And so it was.

This was perhaps the hottest day of the journey so far, and the dehydration effect was very noticeable. Having no pack, I had also no water-bottle; on this occasion, however, I was not particularly concerned, as the village I was making for, Beaufort-sur-Gervanne, if the map was anything to go by, was quite big enough to sport a café or two, and so it proved; I poured a litre of vichy down my throat very quickly, watched in unfeigned surprise by a vast and somnolent St Bernard which was clearly the familiar of the café.

When I stepped out into the mid-day sun, I thought the St Bernard would faint away with amazement; I gave it a friendly wave, in the vague hope that if I collapsed with heat-stroke on the way home – a stretch of some eight or nine miles – it might come looking for me with a bottle of Badoit round its neck, and started down the hill.

'Started' was the right word. With my lack of a sense of direction goes an inability to read the contours on a map, and the downhill section proved to be very brief. I climbed and climbed, and the road got steeper and steeper; yet the map said plainly that I was going towards the valley, and even I knew that valleys must be lower than mountains. It was only when I had almost convinced myself that I had somehow taken the wrong road altogether that I worked out the reason for the road that went up in order to go down; there was a mountain in the way and I had to get over it before I could descend. The map at once became intelligible; the peak lay between the two arms of the road; I had come up it on one side and must now go down it on the other.

More cut cornfields, untouched by scythe or sickle. The hay here had been baled automatically, of course, by the machine, but the shape of the bales was different from the various types of stook (some of them almost cubes) I had seen so far. These took the form of a Swiss roll; clearly, the machine rolled up the hay in sections, then cut it off and went on to the next section. Well, there cannot be many places in Western Europe, if any at all, in which agricultural processes are carried on with the ancient, pre-mechanical implements. (The previous night I had heard a strange sound as I went to bed, and looked out to see the cornfield on the other side of the road being cut by a combine harvester equipped with headlights so powerful that the farmer-driver had no difficulty in keeping the line straight.)

I had just finished my fattest paperback: *Anna Karenina*, which I had not read since I was a schoolboy. That was during the Second World War, when the entire nation was reading *War and Peace* and *Gone with the Wind*. I, too, read both these books; Margaret Mitchell had written no others (she never did write anything else), but from *War and Peace* I had gone on to *Anna Karenina*, and experienced a considerable disappointment. The adult emotions in *War and Peace* were hard for a schoolboy to understand, but the action in the book was so exciting that it more than made up for the *longueurs* of love; in *Anna Karenina*, however, the *longueurs* of love were relieved only by the even more incomprehensible *longueurs* of Levin's social and religious transmogrification. (I did not then realise that Levin is Tolstoy, and that Tolstoy was writing his own idealised autobiography.) It is not a book for children, even children called Levin.

Reading it forty years later, in effect coming to it for the first time, was as profound an experience as I have ever had with a book. I still think that Dostoievsky is the greater and more penetrating artist – greater *because* more penetrating – and his terrible prophetic vision of hell has come to pass in our century down to the last detail. But the insight into the human heart that Tolstoy demonstrates in this book is doubly astounding; first, because for *anyone* to understand human relationships so completely is, paradoxically, a superhuman achievement, and second, because Tolstoy's own emotional life was so tormented, bizarre and at times almost mad, that the instinctive grasp he had of Anna's predicament, which makes it almost unbearably convincing, is even more remarkable than his insight into the human psyche in general. There was an extra dimension for me in the reading; I even felt that my subconscious must have been tugging at my sleeve when I was choosing my reading-matter for the journey, insisting that there was something in it that I, in particular, needed to know. I was no stranger to doomed relationships; all mine, one way or another, had been doomed throughout my life. And there was nothing in Vronsky or Levin for me to recognise and identify with, let alone in Oblonsky. But Anna's fate – her emotional fate, not her physical one – re-opened a still-raw wound, and in addition, enabled me to understand a corner of the human heart that had until then been a mystery to me.

Another, more immediately pressing, mystery arose before me. The hotter a climate, the more insects there are about, and anyone who, like me, suffers from a phobic horror of creepy-crawlies, must beware, as the thermometer rises, of every crevice in the furniture, every dark spot on the wallpaper, every rustle in the corner of the room. I don't know whether this is common to all phobics, but whenever I have not for some time had an encounter with the enemy, I begin to persuade myself that my phobia has cured itself, only to see the hope collapse ignominiously and instantaneously when I come face to face with one of Them.

So it was last night in the Hoffet house. A monstrous flying beetle appeared, followed a few minutes later by another. Someone picked them both up and deposited them carefully at the far end of the garden, while I gibbered in uncontrollable terror, and was reminded, bitterly and yet again, of the extra misery that all phobics suffer in addition to their disability itself; the inability of non-phobics, however sympathetic and imaginative, to understand what we experience, so that even as we are still shaking with the horror, we have to cope with anything from baffled incomprehension to disbelief and derision.

Incomprehension, disbelief and derision can take many forms; towards the evening next day I had begun to look forward eagerly to the enraged incredulity of my friends at what I had been doing. A friendly goat-farmer and his wife had invited me to join in their work for a while; feeling that an experience so far from my normal life would not only be interesting but would in addition provide matter to leave my friends bereft of speech when they heard about it, I had accepted. The herd, I gathered, was an exceptionally fine one, carefully selected, bred and cared for. My first duty was to drive them down the mountain where they had been grazing, and whence it was now necessary for them to repair to the milking-sheds.

Naturally, I expected disaster. Why should any goat, let alone an entire herd of them, go where I bade, particularly since I had no idea of how to bid them go anywhere at all? The farmer's wife explained that they were docile and obedient creatures and I would have no difficulty; I did not believe her, and in addition began to remember that goats were said to be much given to butting those who displeased them.

I got above the herd and, my walking-stick held at the ready for warding off charging goats, I walked down towards them. To my astonishment and gratification, they moved away from me, down the hill, though they went on grazing. How was I to start a general movement without allowing them to go round me and up again? I remembered my instructions, and clapped my hands; the startled goats moved further down the hill.

I advanced firmly upon them; a general downward movement, grazing forgotten, began. Now I was very close behind them, and could see what beautiful and clearly well-tended beasts they were; their coats were sleek and glossy, their sides plump. Emboldened, I moved right in among the herd, and found that while those in front cried 'Forward', those behind meekly followed on. I waved my stick to encourage them, I cried 'Allez, mes chèvres!', I patted those trotting beside me and turned round *pour encourager les autres*. Could it be that all these years I had mistaken my vocation, and that I had been filling in time writing while waiting to discover that I was a natural goatherd?

By the behaviour of the goats, it seemed so. And that was as nothing to what happened when I ushered them through the door into the pens. For a time they milled about, then quietened down; I moved among them, and began to realise what gentle and fawn-like creatures they were. I stroked some, and they nuzzled my hand; I could feel their warm breath, and the outrage of my friends was forgotten.

It was time for the milking to begin. My goats passed out of the pens into the milking area. This consisted of rows of low tables with a kind of fence along the far edge; on the other side of the fence there were troughs with fodder. The goats leaped on the tables, stuck their heads through the fence and began to feed, whereupon the farmer gently pulled the fence at one end; the slats moved out of the perpendicular, and the goats were trapped by the neck. This didn't seem to worry them in the least; they went on quietly feeding. Little did they know that Levin, the Demon Milker, was approaching them from behind.

This, I felt, was where disaster would set in. I envisaged buckets of milk being overturned, I was sure that the goats, the moment they felt my inexpert hands upon them, would lash out with their hind legs and catch me full in the stomach, at the very best not a drop of milk would result from my efforts.

By no means; a few moments' instruction, and the milk was pouring into the bucket at the pressure of my novice's fingers, while the goat stood, calm and obviously unworried, and submitted to my amateur milking as cheerfully as to that of the farmer and his wife on each side of me.

Rhythm, when milking goats, is all; the goatherd squeezes the two dugs in turn, and when he gets the alternating flow going he finds that the process becomes quite automatic. (The squeezing itself is easily learnt. A fist is made round the dug; the forefinger and thumb grasp it as high as possible and 'throttle' it, thereafter not releasing their grip; the lower three fingers do the rhythmic squeezing, letting go after each jet of milk into the bucket and returning to the grip as it finishes.)

The milked goats went happily back to their pens for the night, where the bearded buck eyed me suspiciously as I ushered them in. I kept clear of him; it would be a pity to spoil things now by being butted. I went into the kids' pen, where the resemblance to Bambi was particularly marked, and the creatures even more tame and friendly. Then I sat down to table with the young farmer and his wife; as we ate delicious goat-cheese, I learned that they were not farmers by family or tradition, but had been students in Paris when they decided to throw up the urban and intellectual life and start afresh in the country. Clearly, it had been a great success. As I left, I remembered that the Prodigal Son had ended up, before his return, looking after goats; he must have been far less good at it than I, because he ended up so hungry that 'he would fain eat of the husks that the swine did eat'. Well, well; some are born goatherds and some aren't.

The river was very low, with gravelbanks exposed throughout; at Saillans there was, just across the water, by the bridge, a little row of houses, gaily painted and fronting right on to the river, which was pure Venice; it could have been anywhere in the Canareggio. I stayed the night in Pontaix, the nearest place in which I could find a room convenient for the start of the next stretch, up to Pennes-le-Sec; next day's weather was very warm but with a breeze, and the scenery among the most beautiful so far. As I marched, I was looking straight down the valley at a prospect closed by a range of mountains, Alpine foothills; beyond was another range, and behind that another, until the farthest one merged with the haze.

I passed a man leaning on a gate, and he said – not as a question – 'Vous allez loin.' I raised an eyebrow; how did he know how far I was going? He made his meaning clear with his next words: 'Vous allez loin à cette vitesse.' I wasn't exactly running, just stepping out briskly, but I realised that to a man whose life was governed by the slow, regular revolution of the seasons, to move at such a pace was unthinkable; probably neither he nor any of his neighbours had *ever* walked fast in their lives, let alone run. John Stewart Collis said in his book *While Following the Plough* that no farm labourer is ever seen running, and the day that John himself ran (he had forgotten a vital piece of equipment, without which the plough-horses could not be harnessed), all he could see was the men putting down their pitchforks, or straightening up from the soil, to stare at him in open-mouthed astonishment; they had literally never seen one of their number on the trot.

Another townee's reaction; I had been delighted to see rabbits, the farmer's enemy, wherever I went, and in good condition, too – the myxomatosis must have passed long ago – and here was a baby one beside the path. When he saw me coming, he burrowed into a patch of grass, hoping not to be noticed in case I was a stoat. I assured him I was not a stoat, and he seemed to believe me; at least, he allowed me to tickle him under the ears, until I moved, when he took fright at my shadow and bolted. I was reminded of my epic battle with the Man-Eating Rabbit of Martha's Vineyard. The rabbit had been getting through the wire fence and eating the lettuces, and I volunteered to go out and confront it in single combat. My High Noon ended in complete victory; I caught the beast in my bare hands, took it to the fence (having earlier found the hole it had used to get in) and sent it on its way. Though it was no larger than the one I had just met, I afterwards maintained that it had fangs a foot long and that I had fought it for many hours before, bleeding from a dozen wounds, I finally mastered it.

I passed another dog, a Great Dane, animals only just less savage than Alsatians, and bigger. This one, fortunately, was limping, with a bandaged front paw; as it barked, I decided that if attacked I would knock the injured leg from under it so that it would collapse. Happily, it went back, growling, to the front door.

Soon, the road began to climb steeply, towards Pennes-le-Sec. It was one of the kind normal in this area, nothing but a ledge scraped off the mountainside. But how did Hannibal manage? (And manage he did, because this stretch is one that he would have found difficult to avoid; to get to where we next see him he could hardly have used any other route.) The answer was that he went straight up over the mountain, army, baggage-train, elephants and all; as I went on up, zig-zagging from hairpin bend to hairpin bend, I marvelled yet again at the resolution he must have had, and the even more astounding ability he must have possessed to inspire his men to follow him up what at times seemed a sheer wall, for I had no reason to suppose it was any less steep in his day. Easy for him to say 'What are these Alps? They are only mountains'; less easy for him to persuade 70,000 men to believe it. But he did; that, I suppose, is what leadership is.

The river was now far below me, and tucked in a bend of it I saw a ruined house, ruined almost to the point of suspicion, and so picturesque that I thought it must have been deliberately ruined, or indeed built, by a film company which needed such a relic for a scene set in these parts. Three walls were more or less intact; the fourth had crumbled away considerably, and the roof, or most of it, had fallen in, while bushes and creeper had taken it over, growing up and over the walls. The suspicion deepened when I realised that there was no road or even path to it; how did anybody ever live there in the first place? But the sight awakened all those feelings about the pleasures of ruins. Until the Romantic movement, nobody felt anything about ruins except pity that a once fine building should have decayed, or been knocked down. The Romantics changed all that, but the attitude outlived them and their influence, and is clearly permanently fixed in the human mind. So much so, indeed, that we frequently prefer ruins to the thought of what they once were; my first sight of Tintern Abbey – and this is surely true of anyone who goes there – induced feelings of almost unbearable poignancy, the kind that comes at the sight or sound of the highest form of beauty. I was convinced that I would not have been experiencing such feelings if the building had stood undamaged before me in its original state; it would still have been beautiful, but in a different and lesser way. (Would our experience even of the Parthenon be lessened if we could see it as it was before the explosion of 1687?)

The road began to wind down again towards the riverbed, now strewn with giant boulders, real dolmens so large that whole families were sitting on them to picnic in the sunshine, while the water made its way round them as best it could. I rejoiced that this valley (the river was the Roanne) should be so little known and so little visited; the conformity and timidity of most tourists, who fear to leave the beaten track in case they are eaten by leopards or compelled to drink unsafe water, means that vast areas of France east of the Rhône are practically deserted; and this was still high summer.

Now I was embarked on the series of bends that led to Pennes–le–Sec itself; they were steeper than any that had gone before, and reinforced still more strongly my wonder at the army that climbed this way more than two thousand years ago. They also reinforced, rather more practically, the irritation that a walker on such a road invariably feels when, again and again, he turns a bend, looks up and, seeing no further peak beyond the one immediately above him, concludes that he is about to arrive at his goal, only to discover that the mountain has unrolled further vistas, further peaks, further bends, for him to traverse. But the view down the side of the mountain I had been climbing was the most spectacular yet; again and again, I could see the entire series of hairpins, and when a car passed me, going down, as I was on a little promontory jutting over the hillside, I paused and watched it getting tinier and tinier – from a real car to a miniature one, and from a miniature to a toy, and from a toy to a moving speck – as it negotiated bend after bend. That kind of experience is the opposite of the irritating one caused by the never-ending road; and as I watched the car I was filled with satisfaction at the realisation that I had come up all that way, and on foot.

Pennes-le-Sec at last appeared, and with it its extraordinary story. It had been totally derelict, an abandoned village with only one man living there (he must have been a hermit, as there was then no motor-road to the village), when the entire place – land, ruined houses and all – was bought by Charles Piot, the tyre manufacturer. Like some kind of latterday Robert Owen, he rebuilt the houses and installed modern facilities, and gradually people began to drift back to the place and take up residence. He even built a swimming-pool (though it has now to be designated a reservoir in order to escape VAT, and actually sports a sign reading 'Défense de baigner') and demanded that the state should build a proper road up to it, since it was a community of no fewer than twenty-four souls; the road was duly built. He put up a school (at present it has eight pupils and one teacher), a community centre, a Maison de Culture and a fire-station, and he even installed flower-beds throughout the village and engaged two full-time gardeners to look after them. He died seven years ago, and his son took over his respon-sibilities (he does not, unlike his father, live there, though he visits it); on the outskirts of the village there is a bronze bust of the creator of this extraordinary experiment, with an inscription that calls him, as well it might, 'Notre cher Charles Piot, bienfaiteur du village'. When I left next morning, at eight o'clock, the gardeners had already been round the village watering the flowers.

As I began the climb to the Col de Pennes, everything was still and calm; not a leaf stirred, no life, on two legs or four, could be seen anywhere, and the hills beyond shone in the new-risen sun. It was some time before I saw anything move, but when I did I yearned for Manet to come and paint it; two sprigs of purple clover stood side by side, and on one there was a huge butterfly, its wings white with black edges and black spots, and on the other a tiny one with black wings with red spots.

The path I was now on ran cross-country, marked by the red-and-white signs of the French ramblers' organisation, the Association des Randonneurs. This body does the same as its counterparts in Germany and Austria – that is, it marks country walks and cross-country routes, publishes maps and gives useful and practical information and advice. But the conclusion I came to when studying the brochures of the Randonneurs was that the French simply do not walk – a conclusion, incidentally, that can be reached merely by observation, without any study or research among specialist publications. I got the complete map of all the marked routes in France, and realised that to Austrians and

Germans it would appear to be some kind of hoax, so few are the French walking-routes compared to those in the Germanophone lands. On it there were huge areas of the country where no walking-routes were shown at all. Poitiers and Châteauroux stood in the middle of a desolate plain; a gigantic triangle, equally bare, stretched east and south from Bordeaux; a monstrous stripe of white, untouched by the colours of a single walk, ran along the eastern side of the Rhône valley from Mon-télimar to Lyon, and continued up as far as Dijon. On the outskirts of practically every German and Austrian village there are signposts point-ing to a wide variety of cross-country paths, each provided with an example of the colour-code the traveller is to follow, and in many cases with an estimate of the time it will take him. In France, there can hardly be a hundredth of the number of such walks.

With the wide, sweeping views down into the valley that I could now see, changing at every bend, I began to understand something of geology, normally incomprehensible to me. I could see the folds and ripples of the earth, and it was not difficult to think of the hills them-selves as only larger ripples. These were still only the beginnings of the Alps, but as I peered into the distance, range after range climbing higher and higher until they disappeared, I could begin to feel the unimagin-able prehistoric boiling up of the earth that had, after countless cen-turies, solidified into the Himalayas as well as the gentle slopes of Sussex. Waves of earth and rock had frozen at last, as sometimes, in a very hard winter, the sea freezes around the shore, and all that I could see, not to mention the hillside I was standing on to see it, consisted of such petrified waves.

I was still less than 5000 feet high, but the air was noticeably cooler, and I realised that there must be a good deal of snow on these hillsides in winter; to remain up here when the darkness closed in would be a fairly uninviting prospect. As far as I could see, though, there was no skiing at all; I had passed no lifts, and none of the establishments I had stayed in had looked like, or advertised itself as, a ski-hotel.

I arrived at the Col, and started my descent. I was rewarded at once, only a few yards on, by the loveliest, most extensive and most varied view I had seen so far on the entire journey; I am still not sure if I have ever seen a more beautiful landscape in all my life. A huge panorama was spread out below me. On the far edge of it, the hills beyond the valley rippled upwards towards the sky. The lower slopes were wooded, with a variety of trees that offered every shade of green and russet; in the valley itself a tiny village straggled down the middle, accompanied by a faithful river, while oceans of golden corn and lavender-fields flowed serenely by, stopping every few hundred yards to turn themselves into a patchwork quilt. And the light and shade which governed the whole picture combined in a no less harmonious pattern.

I had the view to myself, for although I had been hours on the march since I left Pennes-le-Sec, I had seen not a single walker in that time, though there were several cyclists, all going my way; that is, uphill. What *they* got out of it I was quite unable to understand; walking up hills as steep as these required a good deal of effort, but pedalling a bicycle up them must have been almost unendurable. I began by wishing them all bonjour, and they all felt obliged to gasp out, between pants, a reply to the same effect; after a time, though, I began to feel guilty in thus causing them to spend breath they could ill afford, so I remained silent as they went by.

I thought long about the view after I had left it and was winding my way down; versions of it, though never again so extensive, were from time to time visible from my path. What exactly does a beautiful view consist of, and what makes it beautiful? Obviously, high on the list of ingredients of this one was the harmony of the composition: the way the corn balanced the lavender, the village was set off by the hills, the little road wandered through the scene providing a diagonal. But to think in such terms was to create a giant fallacy, for no one had planned this view *as a view* at all, and it was very unlikely that anyone had planned any part of it in any sense whatever. Was I then particularly lucky in this view? No; because almost any view of a varied landscape, provided it is not marred by hideous concrete constructions or other man-made objects that do not blend with the sight, is beautiful. That is an extraordinary fact; it suggests that the harmonies of nature are so powerful that no matter what instruments they are played on, in what combinations and at what relative strengths, the result will be pleasing. What is more, and more extraordinary still, is that if the man-made objects in a view are not ugly and do blend well with their surroundings, nature absorbs them into the picture and they actually enhance its beauty. The village I saw in the valley, for instance, seemed to be made of pleasant stone, the houses were of agreeable proportions, the church dominated the village without towering over it. But none of the buildings was of any particular architectural significance, and the little stone bridge over the river was a perfectly ordinary one, probably not more than a century old. And yet I was conscious of the fact that if the village and bridge had not been there the view, though still very beautiful, would have been lacking in something, just as it would have been incomplete if the fields had been all corn or all lavender. Is there some kind of entelechy involved, by the workings of which the elements that make a beautiful view have a tendency to come together in the right proportions? It sounds mad, but I cannot think of any other explanation. And it seems to work all over the world, in all kinds of landscape; look at the wilder parts of Scotland, for instance, where a view might include nothing at all made by man's hand, not even a planted field or wood, nothing but a valley growing wild. Look at the New Mexico desert; it is very grim, with the great fissures in the earth and the giant cactuses straight out of travel-agency posters, but it is also undeniably beautiful, yet not only has man left much of it untouched, even nature has denied it anything that, in isolation, would be thought to please the eye or the mind. The view of that valley, which I saw as I came round the first bend after the Col, made the heart lift. Could the harmony which had that effect really be an accident, its elements fused quite at random? When Van Gogh painted a landscape, he may have balanced the parts of it consciously; much more likely, he did so instinctively. All the same, the balance and harmony came from a human mind directed by a human spirit. What, then, about the balance and harmony of a landscape? Unable to get any further with the mystery, I left it there, and marched on into the heat of the day.

The Hôtel de France in Châtillon-en-Diois was yet another of the struggling little hotels, but my room did have a shower that was brand new, and was clearly the type advertised in the Sunday supplements, which are supposed to be easy to install by following the simple instructions. It was almost exactly the same size and shape as a telephone-box, with smart plastic doors that sealed as they shut, and the shower could be turned to any angle, or removed from its fixings to be used manually. What is more, its two taps – one for heat and one for supply – both worked perfectly; I think it was the first shower of which that could be said that I had met since I left Paris.

I took a shower and lay down. I had walked some twenty-three kilometres that day; not my longest stretch, but certainly near the top end of the scale. I was very tired, but there was pleasure in it, and the pleasure was not of the kind that a man on the rack would feel because his torture had stopped. Like him, I felt aches in my calves, my back and my shoulders, but unlike the torturer's victim, I looked back with pleasure at what had brought about the feeling. Of course, there was the city man's pleasure in making a physical effort (and succeeding in it) that he normally eschews. Further, there was the practical effect; I was twenty-three kilometres nearer my goal. All this added up to a considerable feeling of self-satisfaction. But that self-satisfaction was not, I am sure, the real root of the pleasure I felt, which stemmed from something older and deeper. There is a scene in *Anna Karenina*, in which Levin goes out with the peasants to help with the mowing (much to their initial suspicion and embarrassment, it must be said). He takes his place in the line of the mowers. At first, because he is unaccustomed to the work and very clumsy with the scythe, the effort is exhausting, but gradually he gets into the rhythm and in the end finishes the day having truly enjoyed it; not, however, just because he has been able to keep up with the peasants (thus 'saving face') whose normal work it is. Tolstoy returns to this theme again and again; it concerns naturalness, which is to be commended, as against the artificial life that civilisation has brought. Tolstoy argued, directly and indirectly, that a man should rely on his own physical capacity and efforts, as Gandhi (heavily influenced by Tolstoy) argued that each family should spin its own yarn and make its own clothes. That reliance on my own efforts is what I, for a moment and in the midst of all the aids of civilisation, had been practising, and I believed, as I lay and relaxed, that the pleasure I was experiencing came from an attunement with an older form of nature, before there were roads or wheels or organised society or, above all, division of labour. I was reminded of that strange, literally prehistoric, gesture of a cat, which turns round two or three times before lying down to sleep. The action, which serves no practical purpose, is said to come from the animal's long-buried race-memory of flattening a patch among the grass and stalks and leaves of the primeval jungle, which the domestic cat's remote ancestors had to do before they could settle themselves comfortably. I find that theory entirely convincing, and the conviction is much strengthened by observing the astonishing resemblance of a cat to its great cousins of the jungle and the plain. The kitten in the hotel at Sauveterre, which had kept attacking my ankle, did exactly what a lion or a tiger does when it pounces upon its prey; it clutched my ankle with its front paws and teeth, and tried to rip it open by scrabbling against it with its back paws.

For a moment, then, I was back in a state of nature, where the body and the mind were in harmony, and the mind acknowledged the necessity of the body even as the body recognised the equal and opposite necessity of the mind. Civilisation originally rationalised its rejection of the equal role of the body by arguing that only by suppressing or grinding away the body could the soul be seen; *naturam expellas furca . . .* now modern urban man gyms and jogs himself to death in a profound misunderstanding of the partnership between body and spirit. I had long since promised myself that, back in London, I would walk for some part of every day; I dare say I shall keep my vow, but even if I do I know that I shall not be able to recapture this feeling of justified exhaustion.

Next morning, I set off for the Gorges des Gats, which is where Hannibal was ambushed. It was as dark and threatening as Glencoe, a narrow defile with a sheer drop on one side and a sheer wall of rock on the other. Few ancient battlefields can really conjure up for any but the most imaginative or expert visitor the scene of the conflict; Marathon, of course, is the great exception, but the only thing I can remember about Edgehill was that the brakes failed on the bus I was in as it reached the top, and it began to career down the hill backwards, gathering speed as it did so, before the driver stopped this interesting movement by slewing it into the bank. Hannibal's encounter with the Allobroges in this gorge, however, was not difficult to construct in the mind's eye and ear, even without the help of Livy:

> He learned . . . that the pass was held only in daylight, and that at nightfall the tribesmen returned to their homes. At daybreak, therefore, he advanced towards the heights, as if he intended to force a passage then and there. All day he kept up the pretence, and it was only when the tribesmen had abandoned their positions and retired for the night that he put his real plan into action. As a deception, he had more fires lit than the numbers in the camp would need; then he left the baggage-train and the cavalry behind, together with most of the infantry, and led a picked force of outstanding warriors, lightly armed, to the top of the heights above the pass. At first light, the army broke camp and began to move towards the pass.
>
> As the tribesmen began to return to take up their usual positions, they were astonished to see that the heights above them were already occupied, and that the main column of the Carthaginian army had begun to make its way through the defile. For a moment they hesitated; then they saw that the huge column was already becoming disorganised, many of the horses panicking and causing great

difficulties, at which they swept down the steep side of the gorge with the sure-footedness of long habit. The Carthaginians were doubly beset; by the tribesmen attacking them from above, and by the increasing confusion and havoc within their own ranks, which was causing them greater losses than the enemy was. The horses, above all, were the danger. Maddened by the shouts and clash of battle, which were amplified by the hills and woods around them, they stampeded; the wounded ones lashed out indiscriminately, and many of the army perished, along with the pack-animals, by being hurled over the precipices to their deaths far below.

Despite this terrible sight, Hannibal, above the battle, held his hand, lest he should make matters still worse by attacking the attackers. But when he saw that the baggage-train was under assault, and realised that, stripped of their provisions, the army would die even if they were victorious in the pass, he led his men down in a single charge. For a moment, they did indeed add to the confusion, but the enemy soon fled, order was restored, and the bulk of the army filed through the gorge in safety and indeed in silence.

The day was overcast, almost the first grey sky I had seen, though the narrowness of the cleft (in several places the builders of the road had been forced to tunnel through the rock when they couldn't go round it, and I noticed a plaque set into the wall which said that the series of tunnels had been opened in 1910, before which the gorge must presumably have been impassable except by the river below) meant that little light would have penetrated into this gloomy pass even on the sunniest of days. The clue to Hannibal's success came to the surface again; his instinct for questioning all received opinion. The tribesmen believed that night operations were impossible in such terrain, and thought they could therefore safely go home at night. Hannibal's staff may have accepted this reasoning, but he did not. He picked his men with care, as Hanno, all those weeks before on the banks of the Rhône, had picked the detachment that was to take the enemy from behind, also after a night manoeuvre; but once Hannibal had his élite force with him, he could show that a night march, even over treacherous and unknown ground, was perfectly possible for a commander of genius and resolution whose men trusted him and would follow him anywhere. It was the first battle since the crossing of the Rhône, and was a much bigger clash than that one; casualties and losses were very much greater. But the original thinking that had led to victory was now in its full creative

29

30

flood, and the battle in the Gorges des Gats was a foretaste of far greater victories to come.

I followed the road out of the Gorges des Gats as it wound towards the Col de Grimone; it was really one continuous defile, mile after mile of savage beauty. But the beauty, just before the village of Grimone, was beset with man's unremitting efforts to destroy it. In various spots along the route I had seen signs saying 'Défense de déposer des ordures', some of which had even been obeyed. Here, for the first time, I noticed the contrary injunction: at the highest point on the road, with the cliff falling in a gulley more or less straight down to a broad ledge some fifty yards below, there stood a sign saying 'Dépôt d'ordure'. I walked to the edge to see how the permission was being used; long before I got there, I knew the answer. As I looked over I saw that the entire gulley, literally as far as I could see, was one gigantic, elongated rubbish heap, which was plainly *never* cleared. There were huge piles of plastic bags and cardboard boxes, all crammed with garbage (some of the plastic bags were tied at the neck—*ah, monsieur, quelle délicatesse!*), mountains of bottles, hills of paper, an old bedstead, all the detritus of modern living thrown indiscriminately over the side of a road which was one of the most beautiful in France, and beautiful, moreover, because it had been so little touched by man; this precipitous valley would have been recognised instantly by Hannibal as the scene of his triumph, so little could it have changed over the centuries. Men were less sensitive then, but I could not believe that he would not have grimaced at the smell that hung over the whole pass, and that pursued me, even without a following breeze, far along the road.

When I got to Grimone I found that the place at which I had booked was another *chambre d'hôte*, the spotless, efficient home of M. Le Coq. M. Le Coq kept open house for those who wanted to explore the mountains under his guidance; his brochure, which I found in his hall (he was out when I arrived, on a mountain walk with a group of his guests), offered nature rambles, real mountaineering, bird-watching and many another activity that I would reject if offered; fortunately, M. Le Coq was willing to put up transients as well as study-groups. What is more, he had a real bath, not just a *bain-sabot*, and I wallowed in it for an hour.

The conditions were simple, but the place made an agreeable stay, largely because of my fellow-guests. They were almost all walkers, some on mountains, some on the flat, and comprised a wide variety of nationalities, among them a Belgian couple, the husband bearded and

32 The last smile for some time: Col des Aiguilles

piratical-looking, a Dutch pair who spoke a good deal of English and had visited Britain many times, and two delightful Frenchmen, who, when I arrived in the absence of our host, showed me where everything was (including the refrigerator which held the beer). They added that M. Le Coq would be back in time to cook the dinner.

We gathered – the Belgians, the Dutch, the two Frenchmen and I – in the drawing-room, and exchanged experiences; the Belgian couple turned out to be prodigiously athletic walkers, telling me of mighty marches that made mine seem laughably limited, and when I got on to Hannibal the husband showed himself very knowledgeable on the subject, and indeed mentioned Livy in the same tone – somewhere between a snarl and a sigh – that I had always recognised as the mark of those who have studied him at school.

There then arrived a young man (he proved to be Belgian too), who in an earlier day would have been instantly written off as consumptive, though he was plainly in the best of health. The old adjective cadaverous describes him exactly; he had no chest at all, and from his Adam's apple to his waist was perfectly flat. He caused consternation in the group by his habit of talking to himself – not in the usual mutter of those who wish to give themselves exhortation or advice, but in a loud and lugubrious monotone. Each of us in turn made the same mistake; we assumed he was talking to us, and would reply to him, only to find the reply ignored as the monologue continued. When we had all realised that there was no dialogue to be had with him, we continued the conversation amongst ourselves, whereupon he varied his technique in a manner bound to cause even more confusion; he began to switch between talking to himself and talking to us, so that some of his remarks *did* invite a reply, and none of us ever knew which remark fitted into which category. Then M. Le Coq bounced in, looking unbearably fit, and cooked the dinner. I learned that he was not a native of these parts; like my goat-farmers, he had become tired of Paris and sought a country life.

I noticed, with some surprise, that everyone used the 'tu'; *randonneurs* are clearly a friendly lot. Some of them had been there for a couple of weeks, and had plainly got to know one another, even if they didn't before (M. Le Coq's guests tend to return), but the second person singular was also being used between those who had only just met. I had always supposed – indeed, I knew – that the French are second only to the Germans in the formality which surrounds the change to the more intimate form of address, which seems to need seventeen years of friendship and ratification by a court. (It used to be said that a young man in France could switch to the *tu* without permission or further formality as soon as he had kissed the girl, but that must be long since out of date; the young folk of the Sixties must have used the *tu* from the moment they were born.)

Grimone is an odd place, a little like Pennes-le-Sec. It, too, had been a deserted village (not surprisingly, as it was even more remote), but as communications improved, and largely under the influence of M. Le Coq himself, who is obviously passionate about preserving and restoring the countryside (he should turn his attention to the *dépôt d'ordure* just outside the place), people began to move in, though there was no M. Piot to pay for things. As practically every house in the village was a ruin by then, there was a great deal of building, and it was still going on – somebody was even building a little restaurant. The thought of an abandoned village was very strange to anyone from Britain; surely, for centuries no villages in Britain have been literally deserted? Perhaps a few mining villages when the coal was exhausted, perhaps one or two hamlets in the more remote areas of Wales or Scotland (in some of the islands, for instance); it was difficult to believe that any village in England had been altogether deserted in recent times. The answer must be that in Britain you cannot be very far away from shops and services; I remembered the extraordinary fact that nowhere in the country is more than seventy-five miles from the sea, and much less than that from the next village.

I arrived, pushing my way into a stiff head-wind, at the Col de Grimone; 1318 metres, said the signboard, which meant about 1000 feet higher than the Col de Pennes. My progress was a switchback one – I had next to descend on the other side of the pass – but the mean angle was now inclined sternly upwards, and I began to regret the dips which lay ahead of me and meant more climbing to get out of them.

There must have been a wind like the *mistral* up here, because the same effect, of a sky scoured and polished, was to be seen all round. Two houses straddled the pass, both heavily shuttered, perhaps abandoned; as I started down it occurred to me that there was yet another difference between the French and other countries, in the matter of looking at the view, for almost anywhere else there would have been a bench at the highest point, so that the traveller could rest while enjoying the scenery, or enjoy the scenery while resting.

That night I stayed at Lus la Croix Haute, a few kilometres from the hamlet of La Jarjatte, where the Great Trek would begin.

6

Col des Aiguilles –
The Last Gasp

THE GREAT TREK was the crux of the whole project, as I had realised when planning the journey, long before I set out. It served two separate functions; first, it enabled me to avoid a huge, looped detour that would have taken me far to the north (to the north of Hannibal, too) and added substantially to the length of the route. Second, it was set high in a range of Alpine foothills (or low in a range of Alpine peaks, whichever way I cared to look at it), and the next village on the route, St Étienne-en-Dévoluy, lay among the next range, and there was no road or path of any kind between them; to reach my goal I had to climb up one side of a mountain and down the other.

The mountain in question was not Mount Everest, nor Kanchenjunga, nor yet the Matterhorn or even Mont Blanc. I was not planning to attempt the North Face of the Eiger, I had been assured that I would not need to be roped to my mountain guide, that crampons (whatever they might be) would not be necessary, that ice-axes, oxygen-cylinders and specifics against snow-blindness could safely be left behind. And no Yeti had been seen in these parts for many years. All I needed, I was assured, was good boots. These I had.

A gentle Sunday afternoon ramble in the countryside, then, with a moderately steep patch towards the middle? Not quite. The Col des Aiguilles – the top of the climb – was some 6500 feet high; La Jarjatte was some 2000 feet lower. The track I would be following was marked by the *randonneurs*, and provided that I kept the red-and-white paint splashes in view I could not get lost; even if I did *not* keep them in view my guide certainly would. But I was now looking at the Col through binoculars, and two things were immediately and uncomfortably clear. First, the second half of the route wound its way among loose rock. Second, the Col itself, bare and jagged, looked like a sheer face hung between two posts; that, after all, was why it was called the Col des Aiguilles. It might not be dangerous (though then again, it might); it was clearly going to be, for me at any rate, exhausting.

And there was another matter. For the experts, and presumably for the inexpert and vigorous young, it was possible, by starting early in the morning, to get over the Col des Aiguilles and down to the Col du Festre in a single day. For me, a man only a few days the right side of his fifty-sixth birthday and no athlete, it would not. From the outset, therefore, it had been decided that we would camp on the other side of the Col des Aiguilles, and embark on the downward half of the journey the following morning. I had not spent a night under canvas for some forty years, and had not enjoyed it at all even then; no doubt tents, like rucksacks, had improved since those days, but I did not expect it to be much fun. Moreover, because the only suitably flat terrain was immediately beyond the crest, I was assured that it would be very cold. And what if it rained? And what if there *were* Yetis, or grizzly bears, or wolves, or the ghosts of Hannibal's elephants? And, while I was thinking about the zoological problems, what about the donkeys? For the decision to camp on the mountain meant that a donkey would be required to carry the gear. It so chanced that the donkey engaged for the task was a female one; she had given birth only a month before to a foal, which would certainly have to come with its mother. If there was one thing I knew about donkeys (and there was *only* one thing) it was that they kicked; the combination of a foal that would kick because it was young and carefree, and a mother that would kick from suspicion that someone might harm her offspring, gave promise of broken bones, of a particularly vigorous kick delivered when I was teetering on a precipice, of bruises at the very least; and then, don't donkeys bite as well as kick?

I had met the guide, an affable, shrewd and interesting man, called Philippe; I had also met Stefan, the donkey expert, who dressed in amazing clothes that made him look as though he would be more at home in Carnaby Street with a joint than on a French mountain with a mad Englishman. For both of them, it was all in a day's work; Philippe told me that he was a guide during the summer and a ski-instructor in the winter, and Stefan simply hired out his donkeys for any legitimate purpose. Philippe was interested in my strange project, and thought it most commendable; Stefan kept his thoughts to himself, though he was clearly of the opinion that it would all end in tears.

Was Stefan right? Or, to put it another way, it was not too late to call off the expedition, and trudge round the detour. Should I face reality and blow the whistle?

No. I knew that this whole journey in Hannibal's footsteps had been, from the start, more than a test. It was a *memento vitae*, a declaration that I could still defy the cormorant devouring time. And I was now trapped; I knew perfectly well that the test I had set was a vain one, that if I wanted to reassure myself that I was alive I should find that reassurance within, not seek it outside. I knew now that even if I were to hop up the mountain on one leg and down it on the other, if I were to carry the donkey on my back, foal and all, and cross the mountain thus burdened, singing all the way, if I were to celebrate my arrival in the valley by breaking world records for running and jumping, it would make no difference. I had long known that there was a world elsewhere; now I realised that there were two. The one that lay on the other side of the mountain was far less important than the one I would carry with me up the mountain and down again. But it did exist, and I must now explore it.

I met the donkey, and its foal, which was something straight out of the more sentimental works of Disney. The Palm Sunday cross on its coat was very distinct, and the fur a lovely pale beige, and although the creature was not exactly domesticated, and would not rub itself against me, cat-like, as the goats had when they ceased to be alarmed, I was allowed to pat and even stroke it; certainly it was as warm as a cat.

Stefan had arrived at the rendezvous looking more exotic than ever; he had added a gipsy hat to his outfit. Philippe came equipped with a real alpenstock and a stout rope coiled expertly round his chest; he explained that neither would be necessary, but he would never go on even the simplest expedition without them.

We set off. As we did so, the sky was overcast, and in places the clouds were very dark; surely it wasn't going to rain on this day of all days? No; the sun came strongly out, and soon a little cooling rain would have been welcome. The first half of the climb, though steep, was pleasant enough; we were going through wooded country, in and out of the sunshine. Then we left the shelter of the trees and began to climb through the rocks; the sky cleared completely, and for the first time I saw plainly what lay before me: I remembered the scene in Peter

Shaffer's *The Royal Hunt of the Sun* in which the Inca King, apprised of the approach of the Spaniards, cries out 'Let them see my mountains!'. In the original production, there was a crash of cymbals and an abrupt light-change on the line, and the Spaniards fell prostrate. Of course, there had been no particular moment when Pizarro and his men had suddenly seen the Andes, though previously unaware of their existence, but there might have been a moment when what until then was a vague, ominous outline in the distant sky had suddenly become clear. So it was with the needles above me; the cliff between them looked now like a tennis-net sagging in the middle, and I realised that sooner or later I would find myself going over that net. Philippe said that in distance we were now halfway to the top, and I said that at least it would be down-hill from then on. 'Yes', he replied, 'but the track is much more difficult on the other side.' I reflected that if it was much more difficult than the track I was on at that point, I was not going to enjoy it very much. 'Courage, man', he said in English, and side by side we went up.

By now we had left all trees and bushes behind, and underfoot there were only stones and rocks. Here, a hazard became rapidly apparent; standing level, I would plant my boot firmly on a rock embedded in the earth a little ahead and above me, then use my stick to lever myself up to it to repeat the process. More and more frequently, however, I was finding that my rock of ages was by no means embedded firmly, but was merely lying deceptively on the surface, so that as I put my weight on it it would tip or slide.

Several times I fell, not seriously; but once, the donkey ahead dislodged a big stone which came bouncing down the path to land with a horrible thud on my left foot. My first thought, from the sound and the pain, was that it must have broken every one of my toes; my second thought was that my first thought must have been right. I sat down. After some time, I ventured to wriggle such toes as had any feeling in them; there was no rattling of detached bones. Should I laboriously unlace my boot and remove it, then take off my sock and inspect the damage? But what good would that do? The only test was whether I could walk, and after a rest I found that I could, though limping. Philippe became even more attentive; every time I swayed on a teetering rock and looked as though I was going to topple backwards, he would grab my hand and heave me up. Eventually, we decided that he was my ski-lift, and he asked if I had a ticket; I replied that I had an *abonnement*.

Now there was nothing between us and the pass, which looked more forbiddingly vertical than ever. It also looked nearer, though, and I was astonished and dismayed when Philippe said that it was an optical illusion, and that what looked to me like a few hundred yards would in fact take us an hour.

It took me an hour and a half, and they were the most exhausting ninety minutes I had ever spent in my life; I avoided the thought of surrender only by telling myself that I might as well go on up because it was very much further to go back down, and not a lot less difficult either.

Donkeys, I had always believed, were sure-footed; on this terrain, they needed to be. The mother was surprisingly tractable, carrying her load of camping gear docilely; her foal, who naturally carried nothing, was no trouble, for wherever she went he would follow, though he was curiously reluctant to get his feet wet. Crossing the stream near the beginning of the climb he had hung back until he realised that if he didn't get over soon his mother would be almost out of sight, where-upon he skipped, looking more fawn-like than ever, from one stepping-stone to another, and landed safely on the farther shore. But the donkeys had to rest; not that we had any choice in the matter, for the mother stopped when she felt like it, and nothing could make her continue until she and her infant were ready to proceed. The convoy therefore proceeded at the speed of the slowest member; for me, not an unwelcome development.

The final stretch was the worst, and not only because real exhaustion was now setting in. There had long been nothing that could be called a track, only a picking of our way among the stones, and our course grew steeper and steeper. I said to myself that the view from the top had better be worth it, though long before I got there I had concluded that there was no view, actual or conceivable, that could possibly be worth it. I progressed more and more slowly, bent double now, as that was the only way I could lever myself up another couple of feet. The cruellest blow was yet to come; that trick mountains play on hairpin bends – unrolling a fresh height above the climber every time he thinks he has arrived at the top – was duplicated here. Surely *that*, just ahead of me, was the summit? Only for a few more yards, then another, higher, ridge became visible beyond it. Well, surely that must be the last? Only for a few more yards ... This path, I decided, had as many false conclusions as a Beethoven symphony, and the simile cheered me up, because I concluded that if I could think of so literary a conceit in the condition I was now in, I must have an ounce or two more strength left, and might therefore make it to the top after all.

Suddenly, the rocks stopped, and there was earth, hard but real, beneath my feet, covered with soft coarse grass. I raised my eyes; before me lay a gentle upward slope, and beyond it was the sky. Beethoven had ended his symphony at last, and only twenty paces separated me from the summit. Waving my stick, I charged forward, and as I crested the edge I saw a sight so unexpected that I stopped as abruptly as if I had walked into a wall. Before my feet, stretching right across the opening of the pass between the two needles, lay a huge bank of hard-packed snow. It was filthy – obviously it was last winter's that, lying in a hollow, had never melted – and at first I thought it was ice, indeed a miniature glacier; when I ventured, on tiptoe, towards the middle, I found that it crunched reassuringly beneath my feet. From my vantage-point in the middle of the snowbank, I gazed down the valley on the other side, first looking about carefully in case Brünnhilde might be lying asleep on the snowbank; I wouldn't have wanted to tread on her.

The view *was* worth it. Though the light was now beginning to die, the clouds had gone, and at the end of the valley the mountains rolled away towards Italy; the last one that could be clearly seen was dappled with snow. The hills themselves were mostly bare; there was a little grass and scrub to be seen, but mostly they were rough crags reaching to the sky. I turned round and strolled back across the snow, back over the summit, and looked down on the way we had come. It was a little after seven o'clock, and the bottom of the valley floor, where we had started, was bathed in the last light of the evening, the sunshine that had long since fled from the summit where I stood, and that would soon be leaving the village at the bottom. For a moment, as I watched, the cornfields and the houses stood out, shining in the last rays of the day; then the shadows moved on, and the curtain fell.

I walked back, over the top, to the other side, and looked again at the infinite vista; there was no sun at all here, and the cold was savage. But the combination of the bare climb I had achieved, ending in the view on the other side of the pass and the view down the way we had come (which looked so steep and so long that it induced genuine vertigo) would have been unforgettable even if I had been carried up here by helicopter; to have done it on my own two feet, with no help but that of my trusty walking-stick and a generous tug of the hand from Philippe, doubled the pleasure and redoubled it again. And Philippe had remembered to pack a bottle of Armagnac, which did much to warm my now freezing bones.

What had I proved by climbing to a height of a mile and a half or so over very difficult ground with a rucksack on my back? That I could climb to a mile and a half over very difficult ground with a rucksack on my back. A little more; whenever I had felt that I could go no further, I told myself that I could *always* go further unless I subsided to the ground and found myself unable to get up again. And that point had never arrived. I had recognised not a single flower on the way up, and I knew that I would recognise not a single tree on the way down, but for once this was nature and I was among it; apart from the splashes of paint that the *randonneurs* had left there was nothing at all – not a building, not a shed, not a cow, not a hedge, not a telephone wire, not a scrap of litter – to suggest that human beings had ever set foot here. I was not in the Gobi Desert, or otherwise in danger of dying of thirst or exposure, but for once I had got right away from the city, the armchair, the belief that man is only a thinking creature. Hills, mountains, grass, wild flowers, stones, air, a lonely bird: there was nothing else around us, and for a moment there was nothing I needed.

But only for a moment. I had never much cared for Mussorgsky's *Night on Bald Mountain*, but only now did I discover what is really wrong with it: it is far too tame in its depiction, too sunny in its outlook, too merry for its theme. As night fell, so the cold came on; I now knew why that bank of snow just above us had outlived the spring and was outliving the summer while waiting for winter and replenishment.

The beginning of the night was deceptive; Philippe, expert in all outdoor matters, had collected wood and lit a fire, on which we cooked steaks and a *cassoulet*, which we accompanied with a bottle of Châteauneuf-du-Pape (not quite M. Mousset's Fines Roches). Mother donkey had carried her load well, and as I sat as near to the blaze as I could get, I felt that although this was not an experience I would wish to repeat very often, now that the worst – the climb – was over, it had turned into an adventure, rather than an ordeal, so that I was, in a modest way and to my own astonishment, actually enjoying myself.

Then the fire died down, and I noticed how cold it actually was. Philippe got the tents up; he and I were to share one, and I was glad to see with what care he rigged it and tested the double zips that would make it waterproof and windproof. The last flicker of flame in the campfire died down; Philippe, careful of every detail, stamped out the embers; I crawled into our canvas shelter, then wriggled fully dressed into my sleeping-bag. Outside, I could make out Philippe, with a storm lantern, minutely inspecting the tents, tugging at the guy-ropes with the thoroughness of the old breed of railway wheel-tappers, checking the donkeys' tether. Then he came into our twin-bedded room, zipped himself into his own sleeping-bag, and wished me a hearty 'Bonne nuit'. As far as I could tell from the sound of his breathing, he fell asleep in about a minute and a half.

I did not. In the first place, the abandoning of my earlier intention to go to bed in my pyjamas meant that I had nothing at all to act as a pillow; my walking clothes, which I had planned to roll up and put beneath my head, were keeping me from freezing to death. The only things I discarded were my boots, and these had perforce to prop my head. I had never had any occasion previously to wonder whether a pair of boots would make a comfortable pillow, and I dare say that the question will never arise again, but if it does I shall be in no doubt that the answer is No.

In the second place, I discovered that my sleeping-bag was damaged, and the only way I could get all of myself inside it *and* keep it closed was to contort my body into a shape that was agony to think about, let alone to hold for more than a few minutes at a time.

In the third place, after I had been trying for about an hour, without success, to get to sleep, there was an almighty crash above my head, and the inside of the tent was illuminated for an instant as if by a magnesium flare. I concluded that the Third World War had broken out and for reasons known only to the Soviet military planners the eastern slopes of the Col des Aiguilles had been selected for the honour of receiving the first fifty-megaton bomb of Armageddon. By then I was so cold, so stiff, and so sleepless that I looked forward to my impending incineration, and I was disappointed to realise that it was only a thunderstorm.

'Only' a thunderstorm. It was, in fact, the father and mother of all thunderstorms that ever were or would be. The crashing and banging worried me not at all; I had given up hope of ever sleeping again. But a few moments after the first thunderclap the rain began, and a few moments after that it was coming down like a monsoon.

Philippe had done his work well; if he had not, death would have been inevitable, and in a particularly disagreeable form. The nylon fabric held, the zips were impenetrable, the integral design of the tent meant that the water could not seep in as the ground became waterlogged. But that was all the comfort I could take, and soon, as the downpour showed no sign of abating, I wondered whether the tent-pegs would continue to hold, since what had been firm earth when they were hammered into it was now rapidly turning into mud, and would shortly be no firmer than a bowl of *minestrone*. It would, I decided, be interesting to float down the valley inside a perfectly-sealed tent, but I did not exactly relish the prospect. Then a real fear arose to replace the fantasy one. The snowbank just above us must contain some thousands of cubic yards. It was now being deluged by rain which, however cold, was warmer than the snow. The snow would therefore melt. Any moment now, a tidal wave would roar down the mountain and engulf us, situated as we were exactly in the middle of the little plateau just below the pass.

At this point, Philippe woke up. Since not even he could turn back a tidal wave, I felt that there was no point in telling him of the mortal danger in which we stood, but he presently amazed me by lighting the storm lantern and going out, like Captain Oates; when he returned he explained that he had wanted to inspect the tents – not just ours but Stefan's too – to make sure they were still shipshape. I cheered myself up with the thought that if I was about to be drowned, I would at least be drowned in the company of an exceptionally conscientious professional, and diverted myself by deciding to call the book, in the unlikely event of my surviving long enough to write it, 'My Boots my Pillow: Or, He Died with his Gloves On'.

The rain died out; no tidal wave had materialised. I slept a little, with fantasies of waking to find the whole place bathed in glorious sunlight, and reciting *Pippa Passes* to the reverberate hills by way of thanksgiving. Instead I woke with the whole place bathed in a mist so thick that even the old London particular could not have competed with it for impenetrability; I decided to postpone the recitation, at least until we had devised some way of getting down. It was not clear how this was to be done; even the phlegmatic Stefan was dubious, and only Philippe was sure that we would not fall over a precipice on the way. But I remembered that Philippe's optimism had led him to declare that the ascent would take us three hours, whereas it had in fact taken six and a half; when he said that the descent would take two I doubled it, which proved to be a wise precaution, and an understatement as well.

I was astonished to see that the foal had survived the night; as I listened to the rain cascading on to the tent, my teeth chattering every time I put my nose out of the sleeping-bag, I became convinced that the little creature would surely die of exposure – it was, after all, only a month old. There it was, looming out of the mist, bedraggled but still standing; they must be exceptionally hardy beasts.

During the night, the mother had given tongue, and since I had nothing else to do I listened to the sound attentively; a donkey's bellow is one of the weirdest and most haunting cries in all creation. It always sounds like the most terrible weeping, the sob that accompanies the shedding of the bitterest tears; the similarity extends even to the in-breath, which is full of agonised sorrow, while the cry itself is that of a lost soul screaming a reproach to the very universe. In the dreadful night, such a response was hardly surprising, but I remembered that the same cry had been heard on the way up, while the sun was shining and long before the difficult part of the climb began.

Philippe got the camping-gas stove going, and a pint of bitter black coffee did something to warm and revive me. Though the mist had not lifted, we struck camp; the tents were packed up, our burnable rubbish burned and the rest put carefully in plastic bags for proper disposal down below (score one for ecology), the donkeys were loaded, and we set off.

> Now hollow fires burn out to black
> And lamps are guttering low.
> Square your shoulders, lift your pack,
> And leave your friends and go.
>
> Oh, never fear, man, nought's to dread
> Look not left nor right.
> In all the endless road you tread,
> There's nothing but the night.

Housman's pessimism used to attract me much more than it does now; the melancholic in me responded to it, I suppose. I knew that poem for years before I realised what it was really about, and many more years still before I decided that I could not believe Housman was right. Meanwhile, for the purpose of the descent I reverted to my earlier belief that the poem was to be read literally, and was glad it was day, however misty.

The first part of the descent was easy. The ground, though it sloped away steeply, was grassy, not rock-strewn like the climb, and although we could not see more than twenty yards ahead of us at any point, from time to time a red-and-white marker-stone would loom out of the mist and we knew we had not gone astray. All the same, I remembered Philippe saying, when we had set off on the upward half, that the downward track was worse. Yet the grassy slope continued to lead us comfortably towards the valley; I concluded that I had misunderstood him, and began to look forward to my lunch. The mist lifted a little, though the sun stayed hidden; the turf was springy beneath my feet, I *had* misunderstood Philippe, and the worst was now behind us.

Oh, no, it wasn't. Cassandra had spoken truly, and I had not mis-understood her message; I was about to find out that the worst stretch of the whole expedition, not excluding the last, murderous climb to the pass, the view and the snow, lay in wait for us only a few moments away.

We came to a sheer drop, a cliff that fell away abruptly for perhaps two hundred feet. There was no way over it except for birds, but the red-and-white markers had thought of that, and took us off to the right. What I could not see was where the track was leading, because the view before us was closed by what looked like a massive stone wall, and the cliff ran right to the foot of it. Was I now to climb a stone wall?

I got to the foot of it, and realised that that was indeed what I had to do. The stone cliff tilted to the left; it was therefore necessary to scramble up it diagonally, when the scrambler would find that it curved round, leading to open country beyond. Up, then, I went, heaving myself from ledge to ledge; once round the cliff, I found that the ground levelled out.

It stayed level, but the cliff closed in again, and eventually I found myself walking on a path not more than nine inches wide, with the cliff on my right and the drop on my left. I made the mistake of looking over, and was instantly paralysed with vertigo; I shrank into the com-fort of the wall, and kept my eyes firmly on the tightrope I had to tread.

The tightrope got more and more stony; boulders strewed the track, each one of which had to be negotiated with double care – a slip would have sent me over the edge, and a wobble by the rock would have done the same; I realised that without my stick, which acted as a third, balancing leg for the tripod I had to become, I could never have made it.

I was sure that the donkeys would not, could not, do so. However sure-footed, they had four legs each, and it only needed a stumble with one for them to go crashing over the edge like Hannibal's pack-horses in the ambush at the Gorges des Gats. I was leading the column on this stretch, and I kept an ear cocked for the sound of a donkey going over a cliff; it never came, and every time I propped myself against the cliff and looked gingerly round, I was astonished to see the beasts still picking their way along the track behind me.

Nothing lasts forever; it is just that the bad things seem to. Suddenly, we were over the cliff, and the path broadened out, easy to follow and clearly downward. Indeed, had I been coming along it the other way I would have regarded it as a pleasant country walk, and only turned back when I got to the sheer wall.

Then I saw the path it joined, lower down, and beyond that, the point at which the path joined the road into the village. Up here, it was still overcast; further up, when I looked back on the way I had come, the mist was still thick; but down in the valley the village lay spread out in sunshine.

In the valley, and into the sun at last. But now my back was showing distinct signs of wanting to give up:

Hath he held out with me so long untir'd
And stops he now for breath?

It would be unforgivable treachery if my dubious spine had carried me over the mountain, through the hideous night, and down the other side to safety, only to desert the column then, when the Promised Land was in sight. There was nothing I could do about it except hope, but after an hour or two, I realised that this was a crossroads; if my back gave way the whole expedition would be over, but if it held, I could surely consider myself cured, for I could not imagine any future situation in which I would be compelled to put it to a more severe test. (It held. All sufferers from back trouble are therefore warmly recommended to try walking over the Alps, with special reference to the Col des Aiguilles, for a guaranteed cure.)

When the party was assembled, I learnt that on the cliff scramble the foal had simply followed in its mother's footsteps, like King Wenceslas's page. It was dry now, and its fur was as soft and warm as the day before; as I patted it, I hoped it was not telepathic, because if it were it would read in my mind the terrible thought that had come to me in the middle of the night, which was that if I could kill and skin it I would have a nice warm blanket to huddle under.

We beached in a little bar at the Col du Festre; unfortunately, it had no food. The nearest was at Montjaur, some way away and well off our route, but it would have to do, so off we went to Les Sarrazins. I was too tired to eat or drink much, and I was certainly incapable of walking another yard, though I had planned to get a village or two further on after my descent from the mountain. I took a room where I was: I was restored by a long, long sleep, an ample breakfast, and the luxury of a taxi to take me back to my original route and a little further along it as a final present to myself for surviving the climb, the night and the descent. So I drove over the Col de Noyer instead of walking, and took to my legs again at St Bonnet; my final thought on the ordeal was that if I had known in advance what it would be like I would certainly not have done it, but that I was glad I had *not* known and *had* done it. I glanced again at the *randonneurs'* guide to the climb, and found a sentence I had missed before; it was a warning that the climb was 'un peu exposé' and should be embarked upon 'avec prudence'. I felt that the description fell short of the reality, and the exhortation was unnecessary.

The views from the Col de Noyer were even more extensive than those from the Col de Pennes and the Col de Grimone. Now, however, I was closer to the high Alps, and the peaks I could see were more bare, more rugged, reminding me of the threatening crags I had seen in Alaska, of all places, surrounding Anchorage like an investing army. But on the drive, at the point where I rejoined the original route, I could see that last stretch of the descent, now shining in the sun and scraping the sky, and I gasped in disbelief at the thought that I had got down even that much, let alone the far worse three-quarters beyond it that I could not see, as well as the entire climb on the other side of the mountain. As I sank thankfully back on the seat of the taxi, I concluded that I must have been mad to attempt it. Well, I had thought as much several times on the way up, and several more times on the way down.

33 The foal out of Disney   34 Ascent with rocks   35 Arriving at the summit
36 The infinite vista   37 Last year's snow beneath my boots

83

35

36

38

39

Savines-le-Lac – The Mayor's Bed

I WAS ACCOMPANIED for some days by the smell of woodsmoke from the campfire on Bald Mountain. It permeated everything; my clothes, my handkerchiefs, my very boots, my rucksack, my hair. It wasn't unpleasant at all; on the contrary, it was a rather attractively pungent smell, tarry and crisp. There were, I recalled, experts who would undertake to say from the smell of a wood fire what kind of wood is being burned in it; I, who could not tell what kind of wood is on a tree I am looking at, even when it is standing up and covered with leaves, was in no position to know, despite the aroma in which I was walking. I did think of stopping a knowledgeable-looking passer-by and asking him what he thought I smelt of, but decided that it would not be altogether appropriate.

In St Bonnet I learned from a poster that there was to be a Bal des Pompiers the following week. I wished I could stay; I would love to go to the Firemen's Ball, at which the villagers would no doubt enjoy themselves with appropriate decorum (though what would happen if the Mairie caught fire while it was going on I could not imagine). Why is it that in France, though as far as I know in no other country, the fireman is regarded as a butt: the derogatory expression 'L'art pompier' presumably indicates the feeling that any painting done by a fireman must be rubbish. But why? When I was young, a fireman, in England certainly, was regarded as a particularly glamorous figure, and I believe that the traditional small boy's answer to the question 'What do you want to be when you grow up?' would have been, at least where I spent my childhood, 'A fireman' rather than 'An engine-driver'. I suspect the glamour was partly due to the bell, manually rung as the engine sped by; now there is no bell, only a siren, and on the modern engine there are no firemen clinging to the sides, as they used to, for today the vehicle is entirely enclosed. (A friend of mine, early in the Second World War, was called up not into the armed services, but into the Fire Brigade. Because he was not a professional fireman, and was in addition the youngest member of the crew, he was inevitably assigned the lowliest job on the engine, *which was to ring the bell*. He could scarcely believe his luck, and to this day claims that he had the happiest war of any civilian in the land, and wished the conflict could have gone on for ever.)

On the way to St Julien en Champsaur, the country started to soften; the crags were left behind and the hills became gentler, not only less sheer but covered with fields and woods and even some water. But a melancholy reflection kept intruding as I got nearer to Ancelle, my landfall for the night. I had lunched at a little hotel in St Julien; I ate a very good slice of rough terrine, a steak done the way I asked, some cheese and some fruit; and half a bottle of Beaujolais to go with it. Yet I was struck by the fact that it was the first decent meal I had had for a good many days. The point is that it was simple food simply done, and *anybody* can learn to do that. Why, then, have so few chefs east of the Rhône let themselves into the secret?

Turning over the question I began to devise a tentative answer. *Haute cuisine* in France has gone mad, the condition being brought on by massive overdoses of limelight. Many of the three-star chefs – Bocuse, Vergé, Guérard, Chapel (the publicity-shunning Pic is a notable exception) – have become so famous that their *réclame* has seduced chefs without their talent into believing that customers who cannot afford real three-star meals will be happy with imitation ones. The more magazine articles, television programmes and foreign tours the stars star in, the longer the waiting-list for a table at their restaurants, the more self-promotion they indulge in, the more they persuade the public to think of them as once upon a time film-stars were thought of – that is, as some kind of godlike superhuman being – the more they encourage those who believe that if the cowl makes the monk the publicity makes the three-star chef. From the way some of the three-star chefs behave (going abroad for weeks on end to plumb ever-deeper wells of fame, for instance, leaving their assistants to do their work for them back home), it would be easy to conclude that the three-star chefs believe it themselves. Well, no one gets three stars without having worked very hard for them, and if the *Guide Michelin* is not nearly ready enough to demote the superchefs, and indeed if some of these have notably deteriorated in quality since the publicity-machine took over, most of them are still very good indeed. But most of the imitators are very bad; that, however, is not the bitterest irony. The shoe pinches at the thought that if French chefs with only a moderate talent would be content to cook within their limitations, the hungry traveller off the tourist-beaten track would be a good deal happier.

At last, a ski-lift; just above Ancelle on my way up to the Col de Moissière. Not a big one, but the real thing, and just above the top of it a range of hills, the highest of which were still heavily covered in snow. On the hillsides, the little houses were mostly made of wood, very Austrian or Bavarian in character, though some of them had compromised with a stone chassis and a wooden upper storey with wooden shutters and balconies. Those, if we *were* in Austria and south Germany, would certainly have been covered in geraniums; as it is, they were bare.

Passing two old ladies in sun-bonnets gathering wild flowers, I exchanged a 'Bonjour' with them; as I passed, one of them looked at the steepness of the road ahead of me and added 'bon courage' – most helpful. At once, I found I needed some *bon courage*, because from just beyond the bend I could hear the barking of a dog which by the noise it was making must have been both large and bad-tempered. I gripped my stick, ready for battle, and turned the corner, whereupon all was forgiven. The dog was a genuine sheepdog, driving a flock of genuine sheep down the hillside with a shepherdess beside it; the sheep were presumably being taken out to pasture. The dog, intent on its work, ignored me; I forbore to raise my hat to the lady and ask her if she wanted any sheep milked. (I suppose one *does* milk sheep, or how do we get Roquefort cheese? And what do the Italians do about Mozzarella; how do you milk a buffalo? The Danes have solved the problem by making a very nasty cow's-milk cheese and *calling* it Mozzarella.)

More ski-lifts. And, miles from anywhere, hard by the road, a wayside cross. I was familiar with these miniature shrines by now, but this one was strikingly different, for it bore an inscription: 'Guarnier, Henri, 1984'. Presumably, he must be buried here, but surely in France one cannot bury people haphazardly in the countryside? There was no sign of a grave near the cross, and I assumed that he had not been crucified. Perhaps this was his land. Anyway, a much more welcome sight came into view only a few yards on; a sign telling me I was at the

Col de Moissière, and that I had therefore made exceptionally good speed up the hill: the old lady's 'Bon courage' had clearly been a powerful spell.

The hills ahead of me stretched out to the horizon. A very slight haze softened the edges of even the fiercest granite peaks, and when I came off the Col and began the descent, I soon found myself looking straight down through a V-shaped opening in the range, into the valley beyond; it was as though someone had rung up the curtain in a theatre or raised a blind before a window, revealing instantly a complete vista previously hidden from view. Again, it was perfect walking; sunshine cooled by a breeze, beautiful and extensive views, a road leading from time to time through woods, the down-hill stretch following the up-hill rather than preceding it. I was not back in the forest, but if the map had got itself right I would soon emerge and come upon a couple of villages which ought to be able to provide me with a bite and a sup. Looking up, I could see the wooded hillside through which the path had wound its way; looking down through the trees I could see the plain below, with the hills rising all round it.

Before me, in the middle of the valley, I could see a village which might have been Chorges, dead ahead as the crow flew but not as the road wound; unfortunately, it turned out to be only a hamlet on the way, and it had not a single café to its name (which was Les Borels). Just before I could become alarmed, I saw a most welcome sign, commending the delights of Le Relais de Sapet and insisting it was a mere 1500 metres away. Refreshed, I marched off.

In Chorges I stayed at the Hôtel des Alpes, and the Alps were right outside my bedroom window. At least, that is what I would have supposed if I had not the memory of the climb up to the Col des Aiguilles, with its extraordinarily misleading perspective, especially the last stretch up to the summit. The mountains in my view in Chorges looked as though if I opened the window I could lean out and touch them; they would certainly have been rough to the touch, for they were stark and bare, and looked even more completely perpendicular than the washing strung between the needles had seemed when I began the laborious march up to Bald Mountain. These, indeed, seemed almost too much like a picture-postcard, down to the wisps of pure white cloud suspended in the blue sky above the peaks.

Chorges was a nasty, surly little town. There was not a sign of charm, it had no municipal flowerbeds or any other kind of decoration, it was positively dirtier than Avignon, and without Avignon's festival excuse. The Hôtel des Alpes, the best in the place, clearly got up early to make its customers' lives intolerable; the breakfast-room shuddered under the assault of the noise emerging at full throttle from a jukebox. I had never eaten breakfast so quickly, but when I went out to wander through the streets I speedily discovered that I would have done better to stay in the breakfast-room, jukebox or no jukebox. For Chorges had one feature – entirely new to me – of which I think I can truly say that I have never come across anything, anywhere, so entirely repellent. As I turned into the main street, I could hear more of the blaring music. I assumed that either somebody in one of the houses had put the radio volume up as high as it would go and left the windows open, or that somebody in a car in the street had done the same. But then the music stopped, and a voice, coming from the same source, began to address the town with a series of commercials. I looked about for the offending window, and then realised that what I was hearing, though it certainly consisted of advertisements, was directed specifically at the people of Chorges, extolling the bargains to be found in the various shops in the High Street. Had the offender, then, switched to the local commercial radio station before turning up the volume? I walked on, but the noise pursued me; it alternately faded and increased as I walked, and suddenly I had the answer. All along the High Street, and – as I shortly discovered by fleeing from that thoroughfare – all along the shopping streets of the town, loudspeakers were fixed at intervals of some five yards, and it was from these that the advertisements and the musical din were coming. It was no radio station, however commercial, but clearly a service the town provided, no doubt at a fee, for the local shopkeepers and businessmen. I stuck it for half an hour, before returning to the hotel to check out and flee the horrible place. And not just horrible; where else in France or the rest of the world could you find a town so enfeebled and spiritless, so deadened and indifferent, that at the first sound of such aural pollution the citizens would not take axes in hand and smash every one of the loudspeakers? I stumped angrily off in the direction of St Apollinaire; I had seen a little café right on the outskirts of Chorges, presumably beyond the range of the loudspeakers, and thought I would calm myself with a coffee there; to my horror and rage, I discovered that the café itself had a loudspeaker fixed above its doorway. I shouted an oath or two at its proprietor (who obviously couldn't hear me for the din) and went on my way without refreshment.

On my way, that is, to St Apollinaire. Now St Apollinaire was just the right distance from Chorges on one side and from Embrun, to which I was making, on the other, the right distance being a long day's march for each stretch; in this case it was essential that I stayed there, as every other village on the route was too far from either the starting-post at Chorges or the finishing-line at Embrun. Picking my overnight stay from the map always necessitated a check with a hotel-list, and in the case of St Apollinaire all the hotel-lists, and even the list of *chambres-d'hôte*, were uniformly silent on the subject of a room to let. I had therefore fallen back on the admirable M. Bernard, who ran the Syndicat d'Initiative in Gap, and who had promised to provide any help my expedition required. M. Bernard had already been as good as his word, more than once; now I had an emergency for him to sort out. Was there anywhere for me to stay in St Apollinaire? He said he would make enquiries, and he did. The answer was that there was nowhere, but I was not to despair; he would find me a bed even if it were the Mayor's.

And it *was* the Mayor's; M. Bernard, or the silver-tongued M. Bernard as I then at once began to think of him, had telephoned the Mayor for help in the crisis; I deduced that he must have told M. le Maire de St Apollinaire that I was either *un très important milord anglais* or an entrepreneur who was thinking of setting up a massive business in the vicinity which would bring unimaginable prosperity to his village. Whatever he said, it worked; the Mayor had replied that he was himself going away on holiday, but M. Levin could stay in his house for the night, and his neighbour would have the key. The village of St Apollinaire, I realised from the map, was small; still, a Mayor is a Mayor, be his bailiwick never so tiny, and all the mayors I had ever met (particularly the one who wouldn't stop talking at Tulette) were men who looked as though they slept in soft beds. I began to look forward to my night's lodging.

Meanwhile, I had to get there. As the road climbed, I began to get glimpses of the Lac de Serre-Ponçon, above which lay St Apollinaire. After a series of such tantalising glimpses, I turned a corner and found the road leaning out towards the lake; from the edge, I could get an extensive view of the western end. The water was ridiculously, almost impossibly, blue; hills rose all round it, including the one I was climbing, and if it had not been for the colour it would have looked very much like the Bodensee (as the Germans and the Austrians call Lake Constance) in shape and situation. The road wound upwards, and the view uncoiled fresh lengths as it did so. Eventually I could see right to my end of the lake, where there were massive hydro-electric installations, and after another mile or so I was high enough to see most of the other, eastern, end, with the huge bridge across the middle.

Why should a combination – almost any combination – of water and hills be so beautiful? Lakes do tend, of course, to form at the bottom of mountains, from the water that comes down from them and is not run off through a river. But the result is almost invariably beauty. I remembered driving in Norway once, where every hundred yards or so there is another variation on the same theme of water and mountain. No two were the same, and never did I tire of going round a bend to begin another succession of such views.

The lake's surface seemed absolutely still, though there was by now a stiff breeze on my side of the hill; it gleamed and sparkled in the sun, dotted with what looked like seagulls but were in fact the sails of boats shrunk to bird-size by the distance, and I could see something that looked like a miniature marina. The mountain on the other side was throwing its shadow on the water; it looked as though someone had spilt a bottle of black ink on the otherwise blue surface. And here, just another bend or two further, came St Apollinaire, preceded, I was glad to see, by a little restaurant, which sold me the now regulation litre of Badoit. I sat outside and drank it. Refreshed, I made my way into the village to seek the Mayor's neighbour and the Mayor's key. The neighbour, M. Arnaud, had said, when I telephoned him for his address, 'It's a very small village, just ask anyone for me', and it immediately became apparent that he had not exaggerated, for St Apollinaire looked as though it had scarcely a score of houses. I came upon a lady sitting in a deckchair on a little patch of lawn, and asked if she knew where I could find M. Arnaud; she said that she certainly did, because she was his daughter, that I must be M. Levin (the *très important milord anglais*), and that I had fallen well because the lawn she was sitting on, awaiting my arrival, was the Mayor's, and here was the key to his house. The Mayor's bed was indeed soft. Before I slept, though, there was dinner to be taken.

Vindication! The little *estaminet*, La Fennière, at which I paused for the Badoit on the way into St Apollinaire, was exactly what I had been demanding in vain for so long: a short menu, the dishes within the capacity of the kitchen to cook them, and – at its level – perfection. No genius, or even imagination, was required to cook my chicken livers *aux trois moutardes*, nor to roast my lamb *au romarin*, nor to brown the accompanying *pommes dauphinoises* or dress the salad that followed it, nor to keep four cheeses fresh; only the *terrine des fruits* was in any way out of the ordinary. What was needed was hard work, care and integrity, and these, clearly, were supplied in adequate measure by the management (which as far as I could see, consisted in its entirety of a mother and daughter out front and a husband/father in the kitchen). La Fennière was exactly the kind of restaurant that should have a single star for its food in the *Guide Michelin*; in fact, it was not in the *Guide Michelin* at all.

There was something else. La Fennière was not merely the sole restaurant in St Apollinaire, it was the only one for a good many miles around; there was nothing else at all on the way down to Embrun at the end of the lake or at Savines across it. Now that is normally the road to hell, paved with indifferent intentions, for a restaurant; monopoly is bad for the quality of any business, but for a restaurant it is fatal. Yet at La Fennière the fact that the customers would either have to take what they were given or choose between going much further and dining at home, had clearly had no deleterious effect on the standards of cooking and service. Why not? Obviously, because the pride that the Fennière people took in their craft made it impossible for them to become lazy or indifferent. And that is exactly the attitude displayed by Jacques Pic to his craft, which is exactly the same as theirs.

From La Fennière to *chez* M. le Maire was only 150 yards or so (well, the whole village was not much further across), and magic had descended on it while I was dining. The sky was streaked with broken cloud, behind which was an almost full moon, together with a full complement of stars, and the lake far below glittered and shone with the silver light as it had done earlier in the day beneath the golden shine of the sun. I watched the play of light on the still waters, and found I was holding my breath for fear of disturbing it; every now and again the moon would be hidden behind a cloud, but 'the fair vestal, thronéd by the west' continued to play over the surface, as though the lake were insisting that it could see her even if I couldn't. The bridge shone mysteriously in the ghostly light, a line drawn across the water with a silver pencil, and beyond it Savines-le-Lac shone like a jeweller's stock strewn on black velvet for a millionaire customer. It wasn't Garda, to be sure, nor Rapallo, nor even Chicago, but the combination of water with the lights of heaven and of man was pure poetry; even the far end of the lake, to which neither kind reached, now and again gleamed fitfully.

Pure poetry indeed. I thought of the romantic poets, and of painters like Fuseli, obsessed with moonlight and its effect, especially on water; even of Debussy, though musical Impressionism has never appealed to me. The attempt to capture in words or paint or sounds this kind of particularly romantic beauty had gone on since the Romantic movement began, and petered out only the other day, when a new generation of poets and painters and composers arose, none of whom had ever heard of moonlight, much less seen it.

St Apollinaire being a village of hardly more than a couple of dozen souls, and most of the outside visitors to the Fennière having departed, there was no bustle or stir, no coming or going. One or two nightbirds, attracted like me by the beauty and stillness, were lingering on the way home; a pair of lovers went by, too rapt to notice the moon at all; from Savines, on the other side, there was not a sound to be heard; on my side there was no breeze to stir the leaves and no nightingale to celebrate the scene.

Then second thoughts stirred in me, even as I drank in all this beauty and grace and silence. Surely what I was experiencing was the romantic fallacy all over again. What a lot Rousseau has to answer for! We have him to thank, in large measure, not only for the implicitly totalitarian General Will, but also for the theory of the 'noble savage'. St Apollinaire was not exactly awash with noble savages, but as I contemplated the beauty of the night above and the view below, I instinctively accepted the fallacy in the idea of the noble savage and his habitat. The instinct of urban man when he comes face to face with natural beauty is to convince himself that he is sick of urban bustle and stir and wheels and noises and stenches and shopping, and then to long to 'get back to nature', which is pure and undefiled, and contains none of these blemishes.

The uncomfortable truth about places like St Apollinaire is that life in them, particularly in the winter, is much more likely to resemble Hobbes's celebrated formulation of the life of man in a state of nature: 'solitary, poor, nasty, brutish and short'.

There was evidence of skiing on the way up to St Apollinaire, but the village itself had no facilities for the sport. It must be paralysed, as well as cold, in the winter, with inadequate transport and inadequate supplies; the inhabitants must go miles for the simplest provisions, and many more miles for more elaborate ones. I had felt something of this in several places along the route, and looking at the map I was sure I should feel it even more strongly in some of the little places nearer to the Italian border, but I felt it very strongly here, precisely because of the glory of nature in which it was set that night. But nature cares not at all for us, indeed does not know we are here, let alone why. Nature does not arrange its beauty and serenity for us; it is not even aware that it *is* beautiful and serene, because 'nature' is only a word *we* have devised in order to personalise something which is forever impersonal. If someone had driven a fast car past me through the middle of the village, lights glaring, horn bellowing, gears crashing, I should have been affronted; but nature wouldn't care, just as it doesn't care whether we are flying over it or driving past it or walking round it or stopping for a meal in it. The passer-by in winter thinks that the untrodden snow which covers the village is beautiful, and the icy crags glittering in the sun even more so, and meanwhile the people who have to live there all year round are shivering and resentful from cold.

Again and again, I have to remind myself that whatever the horrors of London, and whatever the decline and deterioration in it that has been going on for years and has accelerated recently, these are not caused by the fundamental benefits and facilities that living there offers. No Londoner needs to be rich to be warm and comfortable and clean; on the contrary, to be cold and wretched and dirty it is necessary to be very poor. No Londoner of even very modest means needs to spend hours every day buying food; it can be done in a few minutes at any one of a dozen shops within a radius of a few hundred yards, and no such Londoner needs to traverse seven streets to get to a public wash-house, for he can wash privately without venturing from his home. Nobody will ever convince me that those who lack these elementary conditions are better off than those who have them and take them for granted, let alone that the deprived are somehow morally purer than the satisfied.

There is, of course, an urban fallacy as well. Since we do take these material satisfactions for granted, we pitch our expectations of them ever higher, and in the end we come to believe that if we have fewer than three colour-television sets and two video-recorders and a hi-fi system and two cars and strawberries all the year round, we are sunk in squalor and penury, and the state (or more precisely our neighbours) must rescue us from this unbearable condition.

A different kind of contrast, pointing however in the same direction, could be seen throughout this region. Wherever I went, I had seen cards and posters, many of them hand-drawn, advertising various entertainments, almost all of them of the simplest and most modest kind. Apart from the ubiquitous *concours de jeux de boules*, there were notices promising a dance here, an exhibition there, a supper in a town square, a play, an evening of music. This is a phenomenon that had always struck me most forcibly in Venice, when overnight the pillars of the Piazza San Marco sprout those familiar yellow posters advertising a concert or recital next Wednesday fortnight or a performance of an opera on Saturday week, and the visitor (and still more the Venetian citizen) knows that that is *the* concert or *the* opera for the month. In London we are spoiled with at least five musical events every night of the year, together with some forty theatres and a hundred art galleries, but nevertheless, in the places where there is one concert a month, or even (as it might be in St Apollinaire) a *thé dansant* once a year, the inhabitants do not spend the other evenings playing Haydn's string quartets behind their drawing-room curtains, partly because their drawing-rooms tend not to have curtains, but much more because they are doing nothing at all other than watch television behind where the curtains would be if they had any. For there is yet another version of both the romantic fallacy and the noble-savage theory, exemplified by the absurd fairy-stories Jeremy Seabrook writes about an idealised working class that probably never did exist in the cities and has not existed in the countryside since the time of *Lark Rise to Candleford*. In the standard Oxford Omnibus edition of that masterpiece, Hugh Massingham's preface to the original edition is still rightly included; it is a magnificent example of what might be called polemical tragedy, and he makes clear in the first paragraph that the point about *Lark Rise* and the other two volumes is that they were depicting a world at the exact moment of its passing. Even then, it is only between the lines that we can guess (and only outside the book that we can discover as a fact) that Flora's father was a drunkard, and he certainly could not have been the only one in the village.

We can make the choice even more stark. Liverpool has more poverty, ugliness and bad government than most British cities; but I do not believe that the poor of Liverpool, who must be poor by now in every sense of the word, among which their material poverty is only one, would exchange their lives for those of the inhabitants of St Apollinaire.

Sooner or later, I suppose, there will be nothing but St Apollinaire on the one hand and Wimpy Bars and McDonaldburgers on the other, and then the St Apollinaireans will begin to demand Wimpy Bars and McDonaldburgers, and after a further interval there will be nothing at all but those. How that tide is to be turned back, if indeed it can be turned back, I do not know. But I knew, as I shouldered my pack after my night under the Mayor's hospitable roof, that is was not just cowardice or sybaritism that made me reluctant to live in such a place.

There was, however, something to be said for St Apollinaire, particularly by me. Its dogs were much better behaved than most I had encountered on this journey. I passed several, including an enormous Alsatian, which did not bark at me at all, but watched peaceably as I went by. Twice, I passed one that was sleeping in the middle of the street, and on both occasions it woke up, but instead of snarling (for that is what, in my experience, abruptly awakened dogs almost always do, which is presumably why the proverb was coined) it just glanced at me and curled up to go to sleep again. The only exception, as I was going towards the restaurant, was a small one that was literally in the doghouse, a kennel that looked exactly like a child's drawing of one, with the peaked roof, arched opening beneath it and tin drinking-bowl just outside. The animal's grizzled little face was sticking out of the doorway; emboldened by the behaviour of all the other dogs of the village I greeted it with a cheerful 'Bonsoir', at which it leapt out of the kennel making the most appalling din, snarling and barking and squealing. Fortunately, it was attached to a long chain, but it went to the full length of the tether in its attempt to get at me.

I had seen very few cats anywhere on the march, and St Apollinaire was no exception, whatever the friendly nature of its dogs. It is true that the cat is an urban creature rather than a rural one, and naturally I had been more yokel than townee on this trip. Even so, I was struck by their scarcity. The French, notoriously, are not animal-lovers; they may keep a dog or cat, but they will rarely display any affection for it, leaving to the British such suspect lavishing on a dumb beast feelings more appropriately – in the view of the French *only* appropriately – suited to human beings.

It was a lovely day as I set off down the hill towards the lake I had seen from above by daylight and moonlight. I paused first to look again at the lake; this time the air above it was so still that the surface looked as though it had been polished, and it was even more blue than it had been the previous day. As I watched, a motorboat towing a water-skier cut across the water, leaving a white scar but otherwise hardly troubling the surface.

I arrived at the lake edge; the bridge, which crossed the lake at almost its widest point, must have been almost two kilometres long, but it proved to be very unlike the magic silvery arrow, speeding across the water, that it had appeared from above by moonlight. It was an ugly, uniform construction, without so much as the gentlest curve, in red-painted iron unvaried by any decoration, with a pavement on each side for pedestrians. I reflected that a white stone one, across this blue water, would have been a thing of beauty, though no doubt also a thing of considerably greater cost.

I walked out to the middle and stopped to admire the view. It was not so extensive, of course, as from the mountain vantage-point, but I could see a surprisingly long way – right to the end on the east, almost to the barrage on the west. The surface was alive with sailing-boats, their spinnakers every colour imaginable, as though someone had upended a bag of hundreds-and-thousands over the water; there were also motor-boats with water-skiers attached, and as I stood there, one of these whizzed under my feet like a giant mechanised Poohstick, and instantly came to grief on the other side of the bridge. His skis came off and floated in the water; I wondered if any water-skier had drowned because his skis wouldn't come off, so that he was trapped head downwards beneath the surface.

I abandoned the novice water-skier and completed the bridge crossing; it ran right into Savines-le-Lac, and a late breakfast seemed to me the first thing to seek. I chose a hotel with a terrace over the water, and watched the sport – canoes were very popular, too, as were windsurfers – as I ate. Then, leaving my pack at the hotel, I set forth to explore Savines.

It was very crowded; I had not been in a place so full since Orange, and had really forgotten what crowds were like, just as in Venice I forgot what cars are like. (Staying there for a month some years ago, I made a sortie, towards the end of the month, to Padua, and found myself genuinely terrified in crossing roads, even at traffic-lights, because of these strange metal objects that rushed about on wheels.) There would, however, be no chance of forgetting what cars are like in Savines-le-Lac; the town was one continuous traffic-jam, and as far as I could tell, it consisted of people arriving for the sport as other people, having had their fill, left. (Many of the cars had a boat on the roof.) Savines-le-Lac was the first real holiday resort I had been in since my journey began, and I felt that I owed it to myself to see how one of the many other halves lived.

Not too well, by the look of it; visitors to Savines-le-Lac in the holiday season who kept their eyes turned resolutely lakewards would be rewarded by a combination of sun and water, aquatic acrobatics of all kinds, colour, daring, enjoyment. But those who ventured away from the water's edge, into the town, would speedily discover that the place offers only souvenirs. I have sometimes thought that the world will eventually make, sell and buy nothing but these amazingly unnecessary objects; in Savines, the process had clearly started, and indeed got quite far along. In an hour's increasingly depressing examination, I came upon horrible cow-bells, horrible walking-sticks, horrible balloons, horrible sandals, horrible greetings cards, horrible cotton hats, horrible toys, horrible parasols, horrible rubber footballs, horrible sheepskin jackets, horrible little things for sticking on the bathroom wall for holding toothbrushes, horrible toothbrushes to be held by the horrible little things, horrible shoe-horns, horrible painted china bowls, horrible T-shirts, horrible paperweights, horrible egg-timers, horrible scarves, horrible pokerwork mottoes, horrible hat-racks, horrible earthenware olive-jars (I would have thought not only that people *would* not make an earthenware olive-jar ugly, but that they *could* not, since there is something so basic and so old about the olive and its uses that a jar for them could not avoid being beautiful, but I learned that the secret of uglifying the olive-jar had been revealed to Savines-le-Lac), horrible rugs, horrible woollen slippers, horrible carrier-bags, horrible decorated pencils, horrible bookmarks, horrible candlesticks, horrible mugs, exceptionally horrible lampshades, horrible bellows, horrible salad-servers, horrible ashtrays, horrible decorated soap, horrible bags labelled Herbes de Provence, which are probably not de Provence and quite possibly not Herbes either, horrible necklaces, horrible stuffed animals, horrible lollypops, horrible, horrible, *horrible* ice-cream.

Also take-away pizzas, take-away hamburgers and take-away broiler chickens; Savines-le-Lac was plainly the take-away capital of France, and even the static shopper fared no better, because in the horrible supermarkets there were two potent symbols of what becomes of a town when, under the weight of easy money and gullible visitors to provide it, all dignity, integrity and care collapse. The first I did not recall having seen anywhere else, though I realised that I would not have to wait long to see it everywhere. Certain manufacturers of jam and conserves now pack their wares for sale in a jar with a little piece of cloth covering the lid; the cloth has unhemmed edges, and is patterned with a red-and-white or blue-and-white check, the purpose being to give the product a homely, country-kitchen appearance, so that the customer thinks it is something specially natural or even home-made, rather than the usual mass-produced product. In Savines-le-Lac (possibly chosen by the manufacturers for test-marketing, on the grounds that since in Savines-le-Lac they would put up with anything, a bridge-head could be secured easily, quickly and cheaply, from which the push outward on an unsuspecting world could later be launched) they had gone one better, or worse: the scrap of cotton had been abandoned, and the country kitchen pattern was printed directly onto the tin of the lid.

The other symbol of decay was more literally so; not far from the horrible jam in the horrible supermarket was the horrible cheese, all pre-packed in plastic. A slice of imitation Emmenthal, inside its trans-parent wrapping, could be seen to be thickly coated in mould.

I wandered out of the supermarket, and resumed my search for something that was not horrible; in vain. All I could see was that sad sign, never used except in the doorways of shops selling rubbish, 'Entrée libre'. (The British equivalent was 'No obligation to purchase', but it died out years ago.) I wandered further; I found what appeared to be the only bench in Savines-le-Lac on which a weary traveller could sit and gaze out over the lake. Or rather, on which a weary traveller could sit and imagine himself gazing out over the lake, provided he knew where the lake was, because in front of the bench there was a thick clump of trees, making the water invisible.

The final indignity: surely, I thought, in a resort so single-mindedly bent on persuading foreign visitors to venture into the town and then fleecing them, there must be English newspapers. There was not one to be had, not even for ready money (and something that is not to be had in Savines-le-Lac for ready money must be a very scarce object indeed).

I strode out of the place in the direction of Embrun; there could be no greater contrast with Savines than this town, which stands at the head of the lake at the eastern end. It was difficult to believe that they were in the same country, let alone that they stood on the same body of water. The very Tourist Office was housed in the remains of a fifteenth-century convent, Les Cordeliers, which had been beautifully preserved and adapted; there was a very fine arched doorway, and three other arched embrasures of the same size and scale. The whole town was instantly recognisable as a real place, where real human beings spent real lives. It had a feel of being lived in rather than passed through, a sense of making things with its hands instead of automated machin-ery, a look of building houses one by one as they were needed rather than streetsful at a time, above all a clear impression that the inhabitants did different things for different reasons, and were not all engaged simultaneously in extracting money from visitors. Certainly there were souvenirs to be had in Embrun, but some of them were plainly well-made, and all together they did not suggest that the place was built of them.

High Street, Embrun, was the *rue* Clovis Hugues. At No. 29, there was a charming little ancient stone façade, just below the top storey, a range of miniature arcades, with faces, animals and people peering out of them; the one at the right-hand end contained the Devil, and the one in the middle a lion with his head twisted backwards so that he could see everything going on in the street below. Almost next door to it was a toy-shop; I braced myself for more cheap rubbish, but I was delighted to see that the window was filled with really well-made wooden toys, simple in design and colour, clearly fitted for use, and even more clearly a pleasure for a child to handle. Everything looked as though it had been made by craftsmen – not artists, and not to be confused with the twelfth-century stonemasons who built the cathedrals, but certainly people who cared about what they were making and who, if they had been told that fools would pay as much or more for worse objects, would still have gone on making the better ones. (There was a slight drawback; the toys had a faint air of being too educational, even self-consciously so, like that London shop called Galt's, of which it used to be said that parents were not allowed to buy any of the beautifully-made toys without sitting an examination designed to discover whether they were fit and proper persons to give their children such things.)

From a guide-leaflet I picked up in the Tourist Office I learned that the lime tree I had just come to was a hundred years old; I wouldn't have known its age without assistance, but then, without assistance I wouldn't have known that it was a lime tree either. And just round the corner was a tiny old medieval tower, stuck between two modern (well, nineteenth-century) houses; clearly, the tower had been there when they came to build houses on that spot, and they had seen no reason to pull it down. Instead, they made the corner into a sandwich, and since there are windows in the top of the tower, I concluded that they had adapted the interior to extend the houses, so that one or the other or both of the tower's 'supporters' had a few extra miniature rooms.

I wandered on through the sleepy streets of Embrun, liking it more and more. Here, for instance, was the Café du Commerce, which was nothing *but* a café, and a perfectly ordinary one, yet it still kept the old front, perfectly preserved, and the name on the fascia was painted in that *trompe-l'oeil* three-dimensional lettering. The lettering was clearly

40 Taking a breath before the next climb 41 The real Alps, almost close enough to touch

old, but nobody had thought to paint it out and replace it with some horrible modern dayglo. Perhaps that is the test, the Occam's Razor which separates the Embruns from the Savines-les-Lacs: if something is both attractive and harmless, why change it? Perhaps somebody should paint right across the sky, so that the world could always see it (it could be illuminated at night), a reminder of this principle, in the words LEAVE WELL ALONE.

Such a town should have a cathedral, and here it was, a very noble pile. Four marble columns supported the portico, the marble multi-coloured, a pale red contrasting handsomely with a tawny gold, and the two front pillars resting on a pair of splendid heraldic lions. It had a square arcaded tower with a conical roof, and right opposite the door was the old canonry, with a bit of an original arch embedded in the front wall, clearly older even than the house, though that must have been seventeenth-century at latest. Just below the eaves in the top left-hand corner there was a very lifelike group of a lion devouring a goat. Perhaps it was symbolic, though I could not recall a didactic meaning for a struggle between a lion and a goat; besides, I had by now become extremely protective of goats; we goat-herds and goat-milkers must never let our charges be ill-treated before our eyes, even in marble, and one of the many things I had disliked about Savines-le-Lac was that goatskins were sold there for bedroom rugs, though I wouldn't put it past Savines to be selling 'goatskins' made of plastic.

Inside, the cathedral was very impressive; a giant nave suspended on three huge marble pillars each side, these being of alternating slabs of black and white, and a vaulted roof with the same pattern. There was also a fine rose-window, not quite Chartres perhaps, but very beautiful, and glowing now with the evening sun. Beside the cathedral stood the old square watch-tower, well kept except for the crenellated top, which had been very nastily restored.

A few yards further, and I came upon a tiny recreation garden, the summation of a peaceful family Sunday. The parents chattered, the grandparents sat contemplatively, and the children ran about and played, with only an occasional word of rebuke or caution when they began to get too boisterous. The dogs were all small, the evening was balmy, the other side of the valley (the miniature park overlooked a steep fall, and it had one of those indicator-panoramas, so that each mountain on the other side could be given its correct name and height) clear in the windswept air. I strolled to the edge and looked over the peaceful scenery, bathed now in the last light of the day. Turning round

42 *The peaceful waters of the Lac de Serre-Ponçon*

to survey the human scene before me, I saw a statue amid the flower-beds and lawns; surely Frédéric Mistral had not followed me this far? No: it was the ubiquitous (ubiquitous in Embrun, anyway) Clovis Hugues, presumably a notable *bienfaiteur* of the town. Until I turned round again for another look at the mountains, this scene, I realised, was more English than French, more English than anything. All over England there are these little patches of public garden in the cities, where the townspeople come of a Sunday afternoon to gossip mildly and let their children off the weekday leash in a place where they can come to no harm. And just as I was thinking that, I saw a scene that some of the English would insist could not possibly happen in England at all. At first, it seemed nothing out of the ordinary; there was an old, quavery black-and-white dog, limping about on doddery legs, obviously not long for the world. Suddenly, a small brown dog, much younger, slipped its leash (there was a child holding it) and leaped upon the other. I rebuked this sex-maniac, saying 'She's old enough to be your grandmother', but that didn't deter the rapist, who left his prey only when shooed back to his lead by the child's mother. At that point the scene ceased abruptly to be familiar, for as the black-and-white victim limped past me, I saw, with horror and incredulity, that it was not a female at all, but very visibly male. In other words, I had just witnessed a homosexual assault by a dog; adult its victim might have been, but consenting and in private it was not.

My ignorance of animals is fairly broad, and my hatred of dogs ensures that in their case it is absolute. So I realised that I had no means of knowing whether the shameful scene to which I had just been a reluctant witness was a common sight; certainly nobody else seemed to be shocked, or even particularly interested, but perhaps the adults did not want to draw attention to it for fear of traumatising the children, and the children for their part saw nothing out of the ordinary. There is a story of Noël Coward seeing a dog mount a bitch in heat, and being asked by a child also watching it what the dogs were doing. 'Well', said Coward, 'the little one there has unfortunately just gone blind, and the other one is pushing it to St Dunstan's'.

I had plenty of time to spare, so I sat on a bench and read, and was at once rewarded with a Tolstoyism after my own heart. He had gone to Paris – it was the first time he had been abroad – and had made notes on the plays he had seen – Molière, Marivaux, Beaumarchais. Then he tried Racine – *Les Plaideurs* – and said, briefly but to the point, 'Foul'. He added – I warmed to him more and more as I read – 'The theatre of

Racine and his like is the poetic plague of Europe. Luckily, we do not, and never shall, have anything like it.' He then went, more surprisingly, to see some Offenbach at the Bouffes-Parisiens, and commented 'Pure French, funny, a sense of comedy so jolly and spritely that he can get away with anything.' From the man who (much later, it is true) denounced Shakespeare as the veriest trash, unworthy of serious consideration, that is an enchanting view. Unfortunately, he went on to spoil the good impression he had been making on me by going to a concert and deciding that 'No one can play Beethoven as the French can.'

I suppose the world will eventually have to choose Chorges and Savines-le-Lac or Embrun and Beaucaire. There will be no communication between them, for no communication will be possible, but we shall all have to give our undivided allegiance according to our choice. But what if we have no choice? What if, as certainly seems to be the case, all the Embruns, some much more slowly than others, become Savines, and all the Beaucaires Chorges? If people want more Savines, more Savines there will be; perhaps we should be ready with a verb – *saviniser*, meaning to make something more like Savines than it originally was. How do we persuade people not to want Savines? (To persuade them to want Embrun is useless, because the whole point of Embrun is that it cannot be made, only grow.) How can we make it true that 'we needs must love the highest when we see it'? I have always, in these matters, been an optimist; the Manichee is wrong, and good is always stronger (and, which is important, more enduring) than evil. But of late I had found my optimism under increasing pressure, and in Savines it had a fierce struggle. And suppose it had not been Embrun at the end of the lake, but Benidorm? What faith would be strong enough to withstand such a double blow? I went back into Embrun Cathedral and looked up at the roof; I felt much better.

8

High Alps – An Invisible Breakfast

FROM EMBRUN TO GUILLESTRE, and from there on to Molines en Queyras; I was getting close to journey's end, and even a blind man would have known that he was very much higher than Bald Mountain, and very considerably colder than anywhere, except that perishing night, on the route. The pass into Italy was almost exactly 9000 feet, and since there were only a dozen kilometres or so to go horizontally, the last stretch would be the steepest, and the very last march – from the Refuge Napoléon, where I was going to stay the final night before the summit – the steepest of all, rising some 600 feet in not much more than a kilometre and a half. But a glance at the map reassured me on one point at least; though the path to the summit was hardly a motor-way, still feet could traverse it, unlike the rock-strewn assault course of the climb to the Col des Aiguilles.

On the march, the days had been getting shorter, now perceptibly so. Hannibal left Spain some time in May, but he had suffered delays; the Romans by now were convinced he could never succeed, and they might yet be proved right, for he was dangerously close to winter. By now there would certainly be snow on the passes into Italy; he had already lost more men by illness and exhaustion than he had by battle, and now he could do nothing but press on to save the rest. As it happened, that was his natural style; in military strategy he was a fox, not a hedgehog. But he was not alone; tens of thousands of men, a huge train of animals bearing equipment and provisions, long lines of horses, and still those thirty-seven elephants, could not try to go too fast, lest the line should stretch so thin as to be easy prey for the enemy lurking behind every rock. And now they were racing the weather neck and neck.

It was at Guillestre, when I had driven over the route many months earlier, that I had found ominous signs listing the passes still closed by snow – this in mid-May – and embarked on the detour that was needed. Well, I had thought, they can hardly be still closed in high summer; I remembered a novel called *Snow in August*, but that, after all, had been science fiction. All the same, the closed passes on that occasion, and the thick snow on the only one on my route still open (another inch deep and that one would have been impassable too), reminded me forcefully of Hannibal's predicament as the weather closed in. The exact date at which he crested the wave is the last of the cruxes of his route, but it was either late October or early November, and some of the more unprofitably indefatigable contestants have gone to the length of working out to what extent climatic conditions in the high Alps have changed in the last twenty-two centuries. Not at all, it seems; it snowed then when it snows now. But what if I should find, on the pass, what he found?

Hannibal realised that his men were close to despair, from the privations they had suffered and from those they feared were yet to come. So he mustered the army and strove to give them fresh heart, chiefly by showing them that Italy now lay directly beneath them – so much so that anyone taking in the whole view would see that the Alps were to Italy as a fortress standing guard above a city. He reminded them that when they reached the plateau of the Po they would be received as friends by the Gauls who lived there, and he went on to point at Rome itself; in this way he managed to give them new spirit. Next day he broke camp and the descent began, and although he met no enemy troops apart from a few freebooters, the snow and the difficulty of the track meant that he lost almost as many men on the way down as he had done on the whole upward march ...

The new snow, lying on top of that which had never melted since it had fallen a year ago, yielded easily, both because it was fresh and therefore soft, and because it had not yet become thick. But when the troops and their animals stepped on to it and went through it, they reached the old snow beneath, and – because it was packed hard – they sank no further, but began to slide helplessly on it, like men walking on mud-covered ground. Worse was to come, for as the men slipped on the concealed layer of icy snow, they fell, and in trying to struggle to their feet by using their hands and their knees, they only slid faster still, because of the precipitous slope. The animals were in an even worse plight; when *they* fell, they broke right through the layer of old snow underneath, and there they remained, because of their weight and the hard condition of the old snow, as though frozen fast.

That, at any rate, I would be spared, and indeed as I passed through Guillestre and began the ascent to Molines, the sun was turning the forbidding crags into a land of smiles. On the sides of the valleys there were some extraordinary rock formations; boulders had been weathered away to a conical shape, and on the apex another boulder, egg-shaped, was precariously balanced. The first sight of one, in the distance, made me think it was the spire of a small and rather irregularly built country church; even when I came nearer, it was almost impossible to believe it was a natural formation. Certainly, these strange rocks fitted well into the landscape, which was the ruggedest and grandest of the route so far, and which emphasised the fact that the crossing-point was not far away; I began to think about the fertile plains below, and take comfort from the belief that the tribesmen who inhabited them would welcome me.

I was welcomed in Molines by the most primitive hotel yet, and certainly the strangest. It must at one time have been three houses, all of different shapes and sizes, with their floors at different levels; the result is that I constantly found myself having to go down in order to go up, and vice versa; rather like a customer in Liberty's. In addition, there were low beams everywhere on which the unwary could bang their heads, and in my own room a really tall man could hardly have stood upright at all. The hotel was also full of notices saying that anyone caught smoking would be expelled at once, an even more potent reminder of being back at school than the spartan conditions at the Monastery of Aiguebelle (though the proprietress – or matron, or Mother Superior – looked astonishingly like an older version of Mme Prunier). For the moment, I thought the fanatics of the anti-smoking organisations had been at work here, but I realised that the injunction was not unreasonable, in view of the fact that the whole place was made of wood.

Mme Prunier had told me that breakfast was served between seven and nine; next morning I got dressed and, after following a strange route that led up and down staircases and at one point obliged me to climb through an internal window, I reached the breakfast-room. There was nobody about, and the room was in darkness; eventually, I found a switch and illuminated the scene. I waited a little longer, and decided to go into the kitchen in search of assistance. To my astonishment, I discovered that there was no door of any kind out of the breakfast-room other than the one I had entered by, which led only to the staircase. In that case, where *was* the kitchen? (The room was laid for breakfast, after all, so the breakfast must be made *somewhere*.) I went right round the room again, searching first for a partition that might slide back, and then, in desperation, for a secret passageway. I could find nothing, and turned back into the middle of the room, whereupon a ghostly female voice, coming apparently from nowhere and certainly from no visible human mouth, asked 'Is anyone there?' I decided that I must have walked into a fairy story, and remembered that what people in fairy stories have to do, at any rate if they want to gain the Princess's hand in marriage, is to go along with everything that happens to them, however weird, so I called out 'Oui, bonjour'. 'Bonjour' replied the Invisible Woman, and asked me what I would like for breakfast.

Trying to keep my voice steady, I said I wanted coffee, rolls and orange-juice, and the ghost replied 'D'accord', and fell silent. Perhaps, I thought, the hotel, far from being a primitive and basic little hostelry, was equipped with the most modern and sophisticated computerised electronic breakfast-system: a pre-recorded series of questions ('Y a-t-il quelqu'un?', 'Qu'est-ce que vous voulez pour le petit déjeuner?') elicited the information required through a voice-operated recorder so advanced that it could 'read' the guest's wishes and instruct the computer to supply what was required.

That explanation, though attractive, was implausible, and it still left the mystery of where the kitchen, however computerised, was. I sat tight, since that, too, was indicated by the rules of fairy stories, and waited for the ghostly banquet (see *The Tempest* and *The Magic Flute*) to appear. Suddenly, there was a mechanical rumbling sound, obviously made by the *machina ex* which the *deus* was about to appear. And thus it was, for out of the ceiling a dumb-waiter appeared, and clanked down the wall until it was level with me; on it was my breakfast. Once more, I followed the rules: you do not ask the Fairy Prince his name, nor do you question his gifts, so I took the breakfast to one of the tables and ate it. (The moment I took the tray off the dumb-waiter it rumbled its way back through the ceiling.)

I finished my breakfast and waited a little, in case the Princess should appear, announce that I had passed the Emperor's test without knowing it, and ask me to name the date of the wedding. Nothing happened, and feeling fairly silly when I remembered what the words actually meant, cleared my throat and said 'Au revoir, merci', whereupon the same ghostly woman's voice replied 'Au revoir', and I went forth.

I went forth to take part in a pilgrimage (grumbling that this whole journey was a pilgrimage). Just above Molines there was a tiny, deserted chapel, used only once a year for this ceremony, which went back, I discovered, for some centuries. There had been a holy hermit, St Simon, who lived, near where the church that commemorated him had been built, in a cave in the mountains, as hermits tend to do; he was a very shadowy figure, and modern scholarship can date him no more precisely than somewhere between the twelfth and fifteenth centuries. His name and miracles were still venerated, though, and the Bishop of Gap was to take the service at the mountain chapel. The pilgrims were to gather at the foot of the track that led up to it; they were marshalled and blessed by the local *curé*, Father Bernardi, and I joined the column as, after a prayer and hymn, it set off.

The sun was up, and the crags bathed in the morning light; very beautiful, though having gone over one I had by now learned to regard them with a rather keener eye than when I saw them, earlier, in the distance or on picture postcards. Everything looked fresh and new, as though the landscape had bathed before facing the day, but I felt, as I had since the start of the hill country, that the evening colours were the more beautiful. As soon as I had left the Rhône valley and began to climb, I would look forward eagerly to the long shadows on the hillsides, where a solitary rock or bush might be elongated into a huge monster. Sometimes I had been in the sun watching the other side of the valley grow dark, and sometimes I had been in the shadow watching the sun take its leave opposite me, but as the heat died out of the day, both experiences had that tranquillity touched with delicate sadness which evening always implies.

As the pilgrims began their walk, the heat of the day had not yet put in an appearance; we were on the shady side of the valley (though making across it immediately, to start up the mountain on the other side), and the cold bit deeply until the effort of the climb warmed me. I was surprised at the turnout; the annual ceremony must be of considerable significance to demand the presence of the Bishop, and a couple of hundred people were making their way up the hillside, many of them having come from considerable distances to take part.

Moreover, the walk was to take about two hours, and there were a lot of small children and some obviously elderly people among the pilgrims; clearly they took it seriously, and any who were inclined not to were exhorted by Père Bernardi in the little service he conducted before he started. This was not, he said, an afternoon ramble for exercise and enjoyment, though he hoped it *would* be enjoyable and provide an opportunity for exercise too. The reason for the pilgrims' dedication to the climb, he said, was the wish to strengthen their faith by visiting the shrine of one whose faith was strong enough to enable him to renounce the world entirely and to bear all the terrors and privations of his life on the mountain.

Père Bernardi held several more such services on the walk; I realised that it was a very good way of enabling the participants to get their breath back and the stragglers to catch up. There were hymn-sheets, though most of my fellow-pilgrims seemed to know the words, which were simple and rather beautiful; one of them was a fascinating essay in linguistic ingenuity;

Touche nos oreilles, nous entendrons.
Souffle sur nos lèvres, nous parlerons.
Donne ta lumière, nous brillerons.
Montre-nous la route, nous marcherons.

Tourne ton visage, nous te verrons.
Coule dans nos veines, nous guérirons.
Vienne l'espérance, nous t'attendrons.
Brille ton étoile, nous partirons.

Ouvre-nous la porte, nous entrerons.
Dresse-nous la table, nous mangerons.
Fais jaillir la source, nous renaîtrons.
Fais chanter la flûte, nous danserons.

The tunes, however, to one brought up on *Ancient and Modern*, were feeble beyond belief.

The climb itself was uneventful; there was a very bad stretch at the beginning, reminiscent of the monstrous Col des Aiguilles, then the rocks cleared, and it was a pleasant path through the woods from then on.

The service was held on the hillside, not inside the church, which would have hardly accommodated a quarter of the people present (many, presumably including the Bishop, had clearly come by other routes); a fine scene it made. The sun was high and the grass dry and warm; there were no customary suits of solemn black, but a most bright and colourful array. The smaller children wandered in and out among the crowd as the service proceeded; nobody disapproved, least of all the Bishop, and nobody even minded the dogs that had been brought along and which not only wandered among the throng but occasionally joined in the responses and even the hymns. Père Bernardi assisted, and a young priest, only just ordained, read the lessons. The Mass was in the vernacular, but the Bishop's sermon, in which he, too, reminded the congregation of the spiritual nature of their walk while congratulating them on the climb, ended with the Blessing in Latin, preceded by a careful announcement that the Latin was for any pilgrims who had come from other countries and did not speak French. (This sounded like an echo – a faint one – of the trouble over the Tridentine Mass, for surely the whole point of the liturgy in Latin was that all the faithful could understand it?)

Everybody (including me) had brought lunch, and when Père Bernardi closed the proceedings with more congratulations for those who had managed the climb, he urged us all to eat our picnics and enjoy ourselves in the sunshine, and finished with a ringing 'Bon appétit!', whereupon everyone spread cloths or sheets or coats, sat down, and fell to. It made a lovely and fitting picture; effort, worship and the pleasure of nourishment. The ascetic would say that the first two are the only ones necessary, and that the third diminishes the effect of the second. The Church has always been careful to accommodate the ascetic until he goes too far, but she has always set her face against letting him have his way completely. I remembered on the hillside that when Christ fed the five thousand it took the form of an outdoor picnic.

Pilgrimage is an interesting concept in itself. A couple of hours up winding forest paths is not, to be sure, comparable to some of the lengths that the devout have travelled to worship at a particular shrine. Presumably some kind of discomfort, or at least effort, is required, to remind the pilgrim, as we had been reminded, that the object of such travel is to concentrate everything upon the goal; the goal is not to reach the place of pilgrimage, but to come closer to God when it is reached. To walk there means to go slowly, with time for reflection and growing understanding of the purpose of both the travel and the goal; to go simply (barefoot in some cases) means to leave behind worldly comforts and thus worldly thoughts.

There are many churches (some of the most beautiful Baroque ones in Bavaria, for instance) which are called pilgrimage churches; presumably they act as magnets to the faithful who visit them from afar. In the case of the pilgrimage to the hermit's chapel above Queyras, an extra element had been added by the fact that St Simon *was* a hermit. A hermit, after all, can be thought of as a man who has taken the monastic principle further than the monk himself. To withdraw from the world, not in a solipsistic despair (the mistake fools make when jeering at the monk or the nun) but to seek God more intensely and without distractions, can obviously be the most rewarding spiritual experience of a human life. If the monks at Aiguebelle had withdrawn into their enclosed space, and withdrawn even further into their enclosed Trappist silence, even with the relaxed discipline that the Abbot had told me about, then the hermit on this mountainside had moved more completely and single-mindedly into the same still centre of being. (As for Dostoievsky's Father Ferapont, he goes further still, leaving the monastery for the hermit's life, denouncing his fellow-monks as devil-bestrewn limbs of Satan, and ultimately rejecting even the bread they leave for him outside his hermit's cell.)

The Matthias Grünewald altar at Colmar, one of the greatest of all the accomplishments of human genius, has as its most striking and meaningful section the Temptation of St Anthony, which took place when the Saint had withdrawn from the world into the wilderness. The hosts of Midian prowl and prowl around, in the form of monsters more hideous and terrifying than those of Hieronymus Bosch himself. Clearly, the devils are threatening to tear him to pieces, and the very sight of them makes a visitor shudder. The shudder stops, however, if the visitor looks at St Anthony's face, with its huge, white beard. It is rapt, serene beyond imagining, let alone reaching, by most of us, and we know that his faith has turned the terrible visions around him into harmless shadows, as Klingsor's Doubting Castle crumbles into dust before Parsifal's sign of the cross. I know nothing about this St Simon, but presumably he was animated by something of the same spirit, and whatever the temptations and threats to which he was subjected, he doubtless faced them with the same strength, derived from the same source, as St Anthony.

As I came back into Molines, the clouds thickened and darkened, and a few spots of rain fell. From the moment this journey began there had been, with the single exception of the night on Bald Mountain, no rain at all; I knew that for many weeks drought had threatened all Western Europe, and the few English newspapers I had seen were full of alarming tales to the effect that the entire nation would die of thirst if rain did not come soon. Perhaps, I thought, it was at last time for me to get my old cycle-cape out of my pack; it was so voluminous that it would go right over not only me but me and my rucksack together, and when I put it on and zipped it right up to my neck I could walk in reasonable comfort and know that my rucksack was sheltered from the elements too. But the rain petered out in a few minutes, leaving not so much as a sprinkling of spots on the road, and the clouds swiftly rolled back, not to be seen again that evening.

Next morning, I moved up to the last camp, the curiously divided village of St Véran. Its chief boast is that it is the highest commune in Europe; at some 6000 feet I could well believe it, if only because the air, even when the sun was shining, was distinctly cool. St Véran is physically split by a hillside; below were the hotels, including the Beauregard, where I was staying; above were houses and the church; the ridge could be attained by following the road as it curved round or by scrambling up the slope, across a delightful meadow, alive with hardy butterflies, braving the thin air to dot the field with colour.

A commune cannot live by height alone. St Véran looked to me as though it had become used to struggle, and a not always successful struggle, at that. The estimable M. Bernard had come up for the day to see how I was getting on; we sat in the meadow above the hotel and discussed *la vie des Alpes*.

Hard? Yes, but far less so than it had once been. M. Bernard talked of the days – they lasted until long after the Second World War – when the onset of winter resembled a siege: the villagers, cut off almost completely from the outside world, stocked up with food and fuel and settled down beneath their irremovable blanket of snow until the spring arrived to remove it. (Even now, I had noticed that the little house opposite my bedroom window was entirely surrounded by a bank of cut logs; from the ground to the windows, avoiding only the front door, the logs, their sawn ends neatly aligned, were no less neatly packed five feet high; there must have been thousands of them.)

It was skiing that had raised the siege, and even started a drift back to the village, reversing the growing exodus as the younger St Véraniens moved away to seek wider horizons. (Not literally: the view of the high Alps from this tiny spot among them was one of the grandest of the entire journey. Beneath the blazing sun, the naked crags looked almost peaceful, and certainly not threatening, hardly even imposing. Once again I had to remind myself that they would not have looked that way to an army now trudging in snow.)

M. Bernard was wary about the effect of television, the easy cliché that our world has adopted to explain discontent of all kinds. Discontent, I suspect, comes from the same inner source as content, and those who flee their home town, or their work, or their family, or their country (or their loyalty to it), often find, to their dismay, that the black bird of ill-omen has somehow contrived to slip into their luggage, and that they do after all have an appointment in Samara. When we finished talking of such matters, I raised with M. Bernard what by now I was thinking of as the Edelweiss Problem. I had spent some time on the climb up to Bald Mountain plucking little flowers I thought were edelweiss and showing them to Philippe, only to be told each time that they were not. I now did the same with M. Bernard, avoiding the flowers that had already been ruled out, but he did exactly the same as Philippe, and vetoed them at once. I asked him whether we were still too low for it, and he astonished me by saying that although we were not, it was unlikely that there would be any around us because it is extremely rare. I had been under the impression that above a certain level in the Alps edelweiss grew in such profusion everywhere that the traveller could scarcely see the ground as he tramped through carpets of the things. I felt cheated; to walk right over the Alps without setting eyes on the edelweiss did seem to me to be something rather worse than bad luck.

Well, whatever St Véran's past had been, as far as I could see when I wandered up and down the high road in the sun (it had rained heavily in the night, but the skies cleared with the dawn), the village was now a bustling and almost prosperous little place, the wooden houses nestling into the mountains just beyond them as though leaning, comfortably and well-fed, against a wall.

The architecture of the houses up here (not only in St Véran but in Fontgillarde and Pierregrosse, the villages on the other side of the mountain, along my chosen path to the border) was very odd; I could not remember having seen anything like it anywhere else. Mainly of wood – understandable for mountain architecture – most of the buildings had curious overhanging top storeys, quite unsupported by posts

or anything else, and some of them looked fairly frail. The galleries
were used for drying and storing crops; I enquired what happened
when the snow piled up on top of the overhang, but nobody seemed
worried, and some of the houses looked as though they had been built
that way centuries ago, which said much for the strength of the strange
design. The church of St Véran was interesting; made in rough old
stone, a plaque announced that though restored in the 1950s it had been
built in 1689. That was an odd time to be building churches in these
parts, surely? It was a Protestant area, and the Revocation was only four
years old; many of the inhabitants had fled in the wave of persecution
which followed it, leaving the village, I learned, virtually abandoned.
Yet here was the church to testify that some had stayed, and not only
stayed but made a striking, and presumably very dangerous, gesture of
defiance.

Looking down, I could see the Hôtel Beauregard, made of bright red
wood; it was exactly the kind of hotel I had been looking for since I left
London, and very rarely finding. It was small and simple, but the
owner-managers understood the limitations posed by the remoteness
of the village and the shortness of the two holiday seasons, and had
solved the problem by keeping the place clean and by training their staff
to be efficient and pleasant. The result could be read in the faces of the
guests, who at the Beauregard went in and out looking cheerful,
well-disposed and generally amiable. Even the dog, an aged black-
and-white creature in the shape of a setter (is there a breed of
black-and-white setters, and if so how did they come to be – judging
by this one at least – entirely without the bumptiousness of their red
cousins?), which normally slept in the doorway of the hotel, would
do no more than open one eye and twitch its tail as I stepped over
it.

A problem, not encountered before, arose on my first night in St Véran;
trivial, but most unexpected. Until I got here, I had invariably, before
going to bed, washed both the shirt I had walked in and the shirt into
which I had changed for the evening, together with my socks, underpants and handkerchief. This miniature nightly laundry was made
necessary by my policy of stripping to the barest of necessities the list of
things I carried on my back. In the old days, I practised the same
economy, but my back was younger then, and would carry much more
before complaining; now, every ounce mattered. In those same old
days, I had also found a shirt which really could be hung up, on my

inflatable-torso coat-hanger, to dry overnight unironed but unwrinkled. I discovered that it still existed; I took two with me. Underpants were easy; nylon ones had existed for some time, and the kind I bought were so light that they would dry in a couple of hours, never mind a night. So would handkerchiefs, though I regretted their crumpled appearance. And, as I have related, the problem with the woollen socks I bought was not that they wouldn't dry but that they wore into holes the moment a foot was inserted into them.

Then the problem arose. Compelled to sing the Song of the Shirt every night before retiring, I had just discovered that at this altitude everything remained slightly damp next morning.

The problem was easily solved (I turned on the radiator in my bedroom and hung the laundry over it). But it made me reflect on a question much bigger than the drying-properties of artificial fibres. Wearing the same clothes day after day (by now I was down to my last pair of socks) was a curiously disconcerting experience; the washing was an innocent chore, but I found that donning the same clothes in the morning that I had doffed the night before produced an unease that I felt obliged to sit down and examine.

I normally wear at least two shirts every day, and about half the shirts I own are silk. That demands a regular and efficient laundry service; there is no such thing, at any rate in London, as a consistently regular *and* efficient laundry service, but there are some reasonable approximations, and two of these take care of my sybaritic tastes. The disquieting effect on my way of life on the march came from the lack of any such service for one who moved on almost every day, and the consequent unease was obviously the result of a dependence on it. The problem was that I couldn't wear two shirts a day with never the same one twice in a week. But *why* was that a problem?

I have never seen any virtue at all in being spartan for the sake of being spartan, let alone uncomfortable for the sake of discomfort. The mortification of the flesh may sometimes be inescapable, but I see no reason why it should be invited, though it must be said that to rely so much on the facilities we can afford is dangerous, even if only because of our helplessness if they are withdrawn. I can perfectly well manage for six weeks with a couple of shirts and an invariably crumpled handkerchief, particularly when I am doing so by my own choice and for my own purposes; all the same, I should not be so dependent on my normal conditions that, were they permanently withdrawn, I would be really unhappy.

The ripples spread out further. When I go away, I stay in the best hotels I can afford; when I go to the opera, I sit in the best seats that my pocket will stretch to. Physical and mental comfort are pleasures, and surely harmless ones. The feel of a clean shirt of good quality on my back does me a little good and no one else any harm. I can apply that to any of the elements of my sybaritism, and I can therefore justify my irritation at the conditions in which I have had to live on this journey. But just as the jury are coming back into court with a verdict of 'Not Guilty', the defendant, to everyone's astonishment, announces that he wishes to amend his plea.

There is nothing wrong with comfort, indeed nothing wrong with pleasure itself, define it as widely as you will, provided it causes no pain to others, for pleasure is not a zero-sum game, and there are plenty more good shirts available for those who can afford them. But it gets, or can get, in the way. If the search for comfort remains too long in the foreground, the search for something that is far more important tends to fade into the misty background. The mortifier of the flesh says we are not on earth to be happy, and must therefore take steps to ensure that we are not; his less intolerant brother says we are not on earth to be happy, but there is no reason why we should not be; their wiser and subtler cousin says that we *are* on earth to be happy, and we can be happy in any way we please, but that the greatest happiness of all is not to be found in the pleasures of any of the senses. And he adds, unkindly perhaps, but not unjustly, that sometimes the harmless pleasures of the senses are deliberately invited into the foreground by the subconscious, in order to hide from view the beckoning happiness in the background, with all the effort it demands for its seeking.

As it happened, I had had a model against which to test these feelings; immediately after finishing *Anna Karenina*, I had turned to Troyat's *Tolstoy*. Now Tolstoy's problem was rather different from mine, hardly to be compared with my longing for my chest of drawers and the shirts waiting for me in it. He was tormented by the struggle between the life he wanted to lead and was convinced he should lead, and the life he actually did lead. There was a contradiction in his heart and in his life, and so there was in mine, and I was compelled to face it in this absurd reflection on shirts and laundries. Tolstoy thought he could solve his problem by giving away his land; I knew perfectly well that it would make no difference if I were to give my silk shirts away; my problem was to stop thinking that the silk shirts matter. Well, well; when I set

43 *Rain at last: my cycle-cape comes in handy*   44 *The service on the hillside: remembering St Simon the hermit*

45

out on this journey, I did not imagine that I would finish it thinking about the Brook Green Laundry, and thinking about it, moreover, in kindly and benevolent terms.

In the little *salon* at the Hôtel Beauregard there were some shelves of books in uniform bindings, clearly a set of some kind; I glanced at them, and found that they were indeed a series, called 'Les Grands Maîtres du Roman Policier'. They were all in French, but they included books by many American and British authors, including Graham Greene's *The Third Man* (I was not absolutely sure that Greene, despite the fact that he wrote a good many in his earlier days, would like to be summed up as a 'Grand Maître du Roman Policier'). The French attitude to the *roman policier* is very odd. First of all, it was they who invented it, even though accidentally; Émile Gaboriau (well represented in this collection) was the first writer of what was soon to be known as the detective story. But having invented it, they did nothing with it. It was the English who really created the form, followed by the Americans, who later on developed it into the thriller; this took somewhat longer to cross the Atlantic in the opposite direction, but when it did British authors rapidly began to overhaul, and then to surpass, the American thriller writers. The English perfected what might be called the Agatha Christie type of detective story, to which there has never been any serious rival. (The supremacy of the English body-in-the-library genre is like that of the English crossword-puzzle; American ones, and still more German and French, are beneath contempt.)

The sight of the 'Grands Maîtres' reminded me of that remarkable German phenomenon, the 'Tauchnitz edition'. (It was, incidentally, the first real paperback. The French had always published their books paperbound, but that didn't count, because it reflected only their tradition of binding their own books; the German publishers of Tauchnitz must have hit on the idea half a century or so before the Penguin appeared.)

You can, or at least until fairly recently could, find faded and tattered old Tauchnitz editions in the older and more faded stately hotels of Europe. The series was deliberately designed for the English traveller who wanted something to read in his own language when abroad (at first in Germany, of course, but later on pretty much everywhere). The curious thing about the Tauchnitz books, though, was that the selection process had no discernible policy. Some classics were included, as were some modern romances, but there seemed to be no feeling of what kind

45 Last village: St Véran

of reader the publishers were looking for or expected to find. Possibly, the Germans at that time thought that English travellers would read absolutely anything in their own language. (Perhaps they would, too.) I believe also that the Tauchnitz editions were not on sale in the ordinary way; when I first started to travel in Europe, there was hardly a hotel I stayed in that was not Tauchnitz-bestrewn, but I cannot remember ever having seen one in a bookshop. But to anyone who remembers them at all Tauchnitz conjures up an entire world; I suppose their finest hour was before the First World War, and the Edwardian world that had vanished many years before I was born came alive under my hands whenever I found a selection of Tauchnitzes abroad; I am sure that the Florentine *pensione* in which the characters in Forster's *A Room with a View* are discovered at the beginning of the book was full of Tauchnitz editions.

The Germans also led the way with Baedeker, the first really practical and comprehensive travel-guide to the modern world. Baedeker (there is even an English poem apostrophising him) is, like Bowdler, associated with an era in which he did not live; Bowdler, upbraided as the typical Victorian, was dead long before Victoria came to the throne, as was Baedeker before Thomas Cook was founded. It was he who first put travel on a scientific basis, and he did it almost single-handed for years. His assiduity was amazing; in the early editions, before the firm became a huge international business, the reader can find (before he sells them – good copies of Baedeker first editions change hands now for substantial sums) two phrases, used over and over again when he is discussing restaurants and hotels, that sum up his meticulous honesty. If he says an establishment is 'good', he invariably means that he has inspected it in person; if he has not been there in person but knows through others that it is of the required quality, he calls it 'well spoken of'.

Baedeker is astonishingly enduring; travellers can use nineteenth-century editions with confidence, providing they take some elementary precautions. Many hotels will long since have disappeared, and the prices will be somewhat different, but if Baedeker says 'On leaving the tunnel, the best view is on the right', it probably still is, unless somebody has shifted the mountain, and his descriptions of scenery and where to go to see it at its best are still valid, as is practically all of his potted history. In the end the mighty empire of Michelin drove Baedeker from the field, and since Michelin the number and variety of guidebooks has proliferated, so that however remote a place the visitor is going to, there will be half a dozen guides to it competing for his custom.

Presumably, guide books flourished as travel flourished. After all, mass travel, let alone package-tour travel, is a very recent phenomenon indeed. Try asking anyone of the post-war generation of travellers, to whom flying is natural, when the first regular civilian flights between London and Paris began. Most will say early in the 1930s, and some will give dates in the 1920s. It was 1946.

The old-style English landlady has long since died out, and she went down fighting, refusing to accommodate herself to a changing world. The seaside boarding-house, at which most of my family holidays were taken as a child (and most people went back year after year to the same house in the same town), was a bed-and-breakfast establishment, and the guests were literally turned out of the house after breakfast and not allowed to return until evening. That seems centuries ago, but it persisted long after the Second World War, and the landlady never did see the storm-clouds gathering over Sea View or Marine House. They should have done; the British working class had discovered 'abroad' under the auspices of the package-tour operator who invented the movement specifically for them, with a powerful send-off provided by the feelings and memories of millions of returning ex-servicemen who had seen something of the rest of the world, particularly Europe. When the Midlands car-workers found that the sun shone all through the summer on the Costa Brava *and* that they could get a drink there whenever they wanted one, the seaside landlady was doomed.

The more I saw of the Hôtel Beauregard the more I liked it. In the doorway, where the dog dreamed of the rabbits he had caught in his youth, there was a sign announcing the existence of a 'Guide du silence et des hôtels silencieux', with a symbol, beneath these encouraging words, of a circle with a motor-horn in it, vigorously crossed through. It was nice to think that there are *hôtels silencieux* at all, let alone that there is an organisation devoted to their interests. (Mind you, to judge from the noise the more boisterous of the children staying in the hotel had been making the previous night, a visitor might be pardoned for thinking that the organisation's code was handled with rather too much flexibility at the Beauregard.) St Véran itself takes silence seriously; motor cars are banned from its precincts except for people living or staying there, though that is not in itself such a notable achievement, because through traffic would find, a few kilometres beyond the village, that the road peters out entirely when it comes face to face with the mountains that bar its path to Italy.

Once again, I regretted that I had not brought my camera. Looking out of my window at the view, I found three tiny birds sitting side by side, as though in a cartoon, on the railing of my balcony. I was standing squarely in the uncurtained window, so they could all obviously see me, but they went on chattering and gossiping and ruffling each other's feathers, quite without fear. They looked exactly like sparrows, though cockneys were unlikely to have got this far, even on a package-tour, and in London the sparrows who alight on my window-box take to flight instantly if I approach the window, however slowly and reassuringly. Perhaps in big towns all birds learn to be afraid of human beings, but that theory almost obliges those who hold it to be Lamarckians, and even then they would find it difficult to explain why sparrows, which have surely never been persecuted or eaten in London, at any rate for a good many centuries, should have acquired such a reaction.

9

The Pass – Journey's End

THE FINAL MARCH BEGAN. M. Bernard had warned me that the road from here, via Fontgillarde and Pierregrosse, got worse and worse as it approached the Italian frontier, becoming broken, pot-holed and dusty; he surprised me by adding that the moment I was on Italian soil it changed character dramatically, and became 'un grand boulevard', a claim which I received with a raised eyebrow, as I had certainly assumed that in matters of this kind the French would be ahead of the Italians. He explained that the real motor-roads, over the Montgenèvre and the Mont-Cenis (both strong candidates for Hannibal's pass), were so near that few people, particularly those who were traversing France only to get to Italy, bothered to take this tiny, winding one, so the local authorities felt it was unnecessary to incur the expense of keeping it surfaced. Though he did not realise it, this was music to my ears, for it meant that there would be little wheeled traffic to go past me as I trudged: little did I know then just how empty the road to the border would prove to be, and still less did I know for what astonishing and spectacular reason.

At over 6500 feet, and with the knowledge that I was going up to 9000, I remembered all those warnings about effort in rarefied atmospheres. When the Olympics were held in Mexico City, the papers were full of articles by 'A doctor', in which the author shook his head and washed his hands simultaneously (a considerable feat), insisting that all the athletes would fall down dead before they had run fifty paces or picked up the javelin to throw it. Indeed, a few years before that, I had paid a brief visit to Mexico, when I had been assured before setting out that if I so much as tried to brush my hair I would keel over, lifeless, at the third stroke. Not only did I not die, I experienced no effect at all: if I had not known that the place was 7000 feet above sea-level, I could certainly not have deduced it from the way I felt. On the Col des Aiguilles, which was not much less high than Mexico City, I had not even thought about the matter, though Stefan said that the water for the coffee was taking longer to boil than it would have done in the valley, and I thereupon remembered the curious property of water above sea-level; remembered it, that is, from physics classes at school, in which I had learned only two things that had stuck in my mind ever since. These were the effect of altitude on boiling, and the inexplicable but strikingly demonstrated fact that there is a difference between the weight of an object weighed in air and the same object weighed in water. (Unfortunately, I had long since forgotten which was the heavier, so I suppose it would be more correct to say that I had remembered only one and a half things from physics.)

At Pierregrosse, in effect the jumping-off point for the border, there was the tiniest church I had ever seen, no more than a hat-box with a hat (in the shape of a miniature square tower) on it, and inside it only eight pews. It was without decoration of any kind, though on the pews were carved the names of those in whose memory they had been given; almost all of them came from a family called Fine. The absence of decoration – there were plain whitewashed walls and nothing else – somehow concentrated the feelings, as I dare say it was meant to; I went up to the tiny lectern that did duty for an altar, and turned the pages of the old Bible, then sat for a while in the stillness.

Not far away was the spot where in May the car had got stuck in the snow (which I suppose should have served as a warning that we would have trouble with the passes); I could see now why the snow had persisted there, as I suppose it has persisted just below the summit of Bald Mountain, because both offered a sheltered hollow in which it could remain, untouched by the warm winds of spring and early summer. Even now, walking through the dip as the sun disappeared behind a cloud, I felt the cold bite at once.

Next day, the rain came at last. I would have welcomed it at almost any point on my long journey up to, say, Embrun, where the real climb began, for until then the sun had been hot enough, even with a breeze to lower the temperature, to make me long for a cooling shower. Bad timing, this, but there was nothing for it but to turn to my trusty cape; it kept me dry, though not warm, for the rain was icy, almost sleet, and beneath my waterproof I was still wearing my frail shorts and a shirt that was not much more than a vest. Still, there was nowhere to go but up; I told myself sternly that Hannibal had not once retreated anywhere on the march, even for tactical reasons, and that I could not incur my hero's rebuke by showing faint-heartedness. At one point, I found myself amid a huge herd of cows which were being driven down one hillside, across the road and on to another. I couldn't see the point; they were not being driven down to the valley for shelter, and the lower hillside was just as exposed as the upper, so they would be as wet, cold and cross after their change of venue as they had been before, and the grass was clearly as lush on one side as on the other. A bearded cowman shouted directions at them, and a very intelligent black dog saw that these were carried out, even nipping back up the hill from time to time to collect a straggler. I moved in among them with my usual fear that they would turn out to be not cows but bulls, and mad ones, too. There were some bullocks, but I met no bull, and if he was about he took no notice of me. I wove my way through the herd, and they started back nervously; several turned away up the hill again, necessitating more swift action by the dog. They were making a great deal of noise as they went, bellowing with what I could only assume was the same misery as I was experiencing, for I have never been able to see why any animal other than a polar bear should be expected to enjoy freezing rain if I didn't.

I went on up; the rain got heavier, and I thought even colder. M. Bernard had cocked an eye at the sky and told me that the weather for the next few days would not be good; it was clearly sound advice, tendered by an expert, but there was nothing I could do about it. I began to think urgently about the Refuge Agnel just before the border; a Refuge was what I now needed rather badly, and a Refuge, moreover, willing to supply a Refugee with a hot meal and a bottle of wine. Fortunately, I had already discovered that it was equipped to do so; now there was nothing to do but get there as quickly as my legs could carry me.

For some time I had been passing or being passed by groups of hikers and cyclists, mostly young; I assumed they were on their way to Italy and that they, too, were planning to stay overnight at the Refuge. And soon I was sure they were, and even more sure of my own intentions, for the rain had long ago turned entirely to sleet, and now to snow, first the fine kind that could turn back to sleet at any moment, and then the real thing, huge fluttering flakes, coming down more and more thickly, until I was walking up into a real snowstorm.

Whatever the physiological explanation, it is less chilling to be snowed on than rained; I cheered up immediately, feeling the exhilaration the snow had brought, and at the same time sensing that I was less cold than before. I read once of a Polar expedition with huskies, which were kept warm by the snow seeping into their fur; perhaps if I had paid more attention to the physics teacher I would have understood why some cold things make you warmer.

The passers-by, in both directions, were now dressed in all-enveloping anoraks with hoods, windcheaters, thick gloves and even goggles, and I began to wonder why they were doing it. I knew, or thought I did, why I was doing it, but very few of my young fellow-hikers could have had my reasons. What is more, almost all of them were French, and I thought it was the English who took their pleasures sadly if not masochistically. My surprise increased when I finally arrived at the Refuge Agnel (a night's lodging cost the frightful sum of twenty-five francs), to find a group about to set out, with a guide, not down to Italy but on a circular ramble which would bring them back to the Refuge (where, incidentally, I was greeted by a sign saying that no one arriving by car would be admitted). For my part I felt that once I was through the welcoming door nothing but the most urgent necessity would persuade me to leave; as it happened, the urgent necessity – to cross the border and thus complete the expedition – beckoned, and I determined to cling to the thought of the first cup of *espresso* coffee I would have in Italy; these ramblers didn't even have that warming goal in view, and by now the snow was settling lavishly over everything, including the road, which had long since been abandoned by the motorists.

Inside the Refuge, all was warmth and friendliness, though most of the former came from the latter, as the heating was minimal. However, with the dining-room door and windows shut and about 120 people in a room which would hold half the number in reasonable comfort, the prospect of a pleasant night returned. The young people had something of the air of the *randonneurs* at Grimone, *chez* M. Le Coq, with the additional advantage of their youth, which turned the blizzard into an adventure for them to laugh at. Few of them, I learned, had known each other before arriving here, and most had arrived yesterday, though when they would get away none could guess. I asked them what they did when they were trapped indoors while on an essentially outdoor holiday: 'On discute.' It suddenly struck me that nobody around me was complaining, and since I had already discovered that for most of them it was their annual holiday, and a surprisingly brief one, they would have been well entitled to moan about it being ruined by the snow, and to insist that it wasn't *fair*. Yet there was nothing but good cheer in the room, and I was sure that it was based on the feeling I had sensed among the more mature walkers at Grimone; the pleasure in the company of strangers who share one thing, in this case a desire to walk over France's mountains green, and were not at all downcast to discover that the mountains were white.

The man in charge of this merry *gîte* seemed exactly right for the post; very understanding and benevolent, and obviously very popular with the mountaineers who stayed there regularly. I asked him if snow in August was common in these parts, for all that we were almost at 9000 feet, and he said it was unusual but not unknown; most years, there would be one or two snowfalls in July or August, though rarely as heavy as this. Amid the banter, dinner came to an end, and there was nothing left to do but to *discute* some more and go to bed. I reflected that it had been a very long time since I last went to bed in a dormitory, and even then it was certainly not a dormitory for both sexes.

Next morning, the land was transformed; the snow had fallen heavily all night, and was still coming down. A wonderful stillness was all around; the pass was obviously closed to wheels, so nothing could be heard but the squeak of boots on virgin snow. And that was heard early, because another ramble was setting off first thing in the morning, though the temperature had fallen considerably in the night. Once again, the anoraks were buttoned tight, and the trousers tucked further into the boots; in addition, the bold members of the sortie were all putting what seemed to be a colourless lipstick on their faces; I was assured that it was a specific against frostbite, and began to wonder, not for the first time in the past day and a half, what I had let myself in for.

What *had* I let myself in for? Following in Hannibal's footsteps, I had walked from the Camargue, via the Rhône and the beginnings of the Alps, to one of the highest points in the range, and soon I would formally seal the achievement by crossing into Italy.

My satisfaction was increased by the knowledge that my fifty-sixth birthday was now only a few days away. There were more satisfactions: no insoluble problem had beset the expedition, and none had beset me. I was fitter than I had ever been in my life. No doubt I was mad to hit upon the plan in the first place, madder to go ahead with it in the second, madder still not to give it up after a couple of weeks, and maddest of all to be standing on a road in six inches of snow, preparing to stroll over the Italian border with more snow settling on my hat. If I had known about the ordeal of Bald Mountain I would have obeyed the Great Boyg's injunction to Peer Gynt: 'You must go round' (though Peer didn't). But if I had known everything else, including the snow, I realised that I would still have gone ahead, and I was happy and satisfied that I had. I saluted the heavens, and packed away my cape; I would enter Italy as I had entered France.

In Belloc's *The Path to Rome* there is a passage in which he tells of his defeat at a snowbound pass; he insists that the guide lead him over, despite the man's insistence that it is impossible, and is beaten back by a blizzard which makes him realise that he would never get through alive. He returns to the inn. But he was doing it in winter, like Hannibal; though the snow now lay deep and crisp and even, it was not going to stop *me*.

That was the satisfaction of finishing: what about the satisfaction of the journey itself? The most stimulating aspect of the whole march had been, undoubtedly, the contrasting landscapes. I had started in the Camargue, which whatever else it was was flat, and I had now arrived at the top of the Alps, which whatever they were were very far indeed from flat. In between there had been every other variety of countryside, in the constantly changing rhythms of slopes and riverbeds, thin scrub and heavy woodland, evergreens and deciduous, grass and granite, sunflowers and clover, orchards and meadows, corn and lavender, lush vines and poor vines. Nor had the variety been confined to nature and man's hand laid upon it; the styles of farmhouses had changed, from thick stone walls built against the heat of Provence to the wooden Alpine chalets with their roofs pitched to retain the insulating blanket of the snow in winter and to throw it off as soon as the spring arrived to soften it. Then again, attitudes had changed, not always subtly; off the beaten track, where there were no tourists, where the skiing was unfashionable and where there was hardly a first-class hotel between Valence and Italy, the atmosphere was far more genial. There was none of the pressure applied further south by those who must please transient visitors or go under, for the transient visitors here were seeking different things, in a different frame of mind, from the visitors who fill Avignon and Arles and Aix and Orange and Montélimar and Tarascon.

To some extent this changing character must have reflected the difference between Provence and the rest of the country (or rather, since Provence stretches far to the north, between southern Provence and the rest of it). Up above, there must have been something like a race-memory, bred into the bones and blood, of the time the inhabitants had to fight to stay alive; down below, the parallel memories would have been of a smiling, generous landscape offering fruit for the plucking. Obviously, neither half of the contrast is literally true any longer, but I had a distinct sense of the difference between a land which expected nothing not won by the people's own exertions and an area tempted to think that the world owed it a living.

What distorted the picture was the progressive ruin of southern Provence: is there *anywhere* fit to visit in summer along the Côte d'Azur? Perhaps the Alpine dwellers will have the last laugh after all. Or perhaps the world will change even more dramatically, and agree upon an international convention under the terms of which tourists will be limited in numbers and in the areas they may visit, so that all the earth's people may get on with the job of earning their living in the time-honoured way, even if they are obliged to ask the oldest inhabitant to explain what it was. Is there not a knell for our tourist-laden world in the story of the prehistoric drawings in the Lascaux caves? For at least 20,000 years they had slumbered beneath the earth, keeping their artistic achievements inviolate. Then two small boys fell through a hole chasing their dog, and this astounding treasure was given to the world. And what did the world do? The world *breathed on it*; the thousands of visitors who tramped through the caves caused massive condensation to form in the atmosphere, and in the ensuing damp the pictures began to disintegrate. So the caves were closed, and went back to their silent sleep beneath the earth, though not before every detail of the drawings had been examined, measured, X-rayed and photographed, and an exact copy of the caves and their artistic treasure fabricated nearby, in conditions which would preclude the discolouring or destruction of the pictures, even if only because these reproductions would be done in some plastic, photographic, inert material that would never decay at all. I could not help feeling, when I heard of this project, that somebody had missed the point in a rather extreme way, and I have not ceased to think so since.

Meanwhile, I was standing outside the Refuge Agnel being snowed on, and determined to walk to Italy or perish, or most likely both. There was very little wind, which meant that I was no colder than the snow; I had the mountains virtually to myself; and I could not turn back now, in August, where Hannibal had pressed on in November. Brandishing my stick at Rome, I set off.

Alone in the snow I could face for the last time the last question of all. Why, really, had I done it? Why, truly, had I walked from the Camargue to the high Alps? What I sought might have been behind any hedge I walked past, within any clump of trees I glanced at. But I could not believe that the universe would play such games. More likely it was still beyond the next mountain; or, if not, the next but one; or, most likely perhaps, behind the one that could not quite be seen, hazy and indistinct on the horizon. And perhaps beyond *that* one there is peace and serenity and understanding, and even the answer to the very last question of all: since we must die, why do we live first?

Until now, I had always been looking up at the peaks covered in snow from a valley free of it; for the first time, I saw this monstrous and marvellous landscape from amidst it. In the focus of the view there stood the biggest mountain in this part of the Alps, Le Pain de Sucre, a huge, conical shape looking something like a snowman and something like a child's drawing of a mountain. It towered over its neighbours, stark white with not a scrap of rock showing through; it was difficult to believe that it was not part of a stage set or an illustration in a book of fairy-tales, and even more difficult to believe that this was happening in the hottest month of the European year. It occurred to me at this point that I was wearing a good deal less than Hannibal's soldiers; at least I was not proposing to camp up here.

I toiled up the last hills, as the now invisible path snaked its way towards the border. Juvenal sustained me:

On, on, you madman! Onwards across these murderous Alps!
Thrill schoolboys with your exploits, so that they
May have a fit subject for their mock orations!

Madman indeed; what was going to happen at the border, when I arrived, in a snowstorm, wearing a short-sleeved open-necked shirt, a pair of khaki shorts above the knee, a straw hat with a fancy band round it, socks turned down over the tops of my boots, a rucksack on my back and a walking-stick in my hand? Would it make matters better or worse if I said I was only nipping over into Italy for a cup of coffee? If, asked why I was dressed so inappropriately, I were to reply that it had been much warmer where I had started, would I be more or less likely to be arrested if I volunteered the information that I had started at Aigues-Mortes? And would I be more or less likely to be turned back by the Italian border officials if I said that I was following Hannibal, and added that I had no elephants to declare?

Of one thing at least I could be sure; any interrogation, whether French or Italian, would be taking place inside the border post, not in the open air, for however well wrapped up the officials might be, they would not greatly relish the task of interrogating a lunatic in what by now had become a real blizzard.

I might have known. When I got to the border, it was marked only by a metal sign, practically obscured (I had to thump it vigorously with my stick to shake the snow off), and there was not a human being, French or Italian, anywhere to be seen. Clearly, the Italian authorities did not expect another Hannibal, and the French ones had accepted his assurance that he was only in transit and meant them no harm. Even the metal sign which told me that the border was here did not specify exactly where I would cross it. Perhaps, while Europe's leaders argued in Brussels, Strasburg and Luxemburg, one small step towards European unity was being taken up here. I suppose you could say that the Roman Empire, and the Pax Romana which it brought, was the first attempt to make all Europe into one. But the idea of a united Europe made out of independent and equal states would have been very strange to Augustus Caesar, as it had been strange to all those who have tried since the Roman Empire to dominate the entire continent; Charlemagne, the Catholic Church, Napoleon, and finally the terrible perversion of the idea by Hitler. Now we argue about butter mountains; from where I stood, where Hannibal stood, the Alps looked more impressive.

I marched across the invisible line, into Italy; the lush fields below me could not be seen, but I believed they were there. The alliances, the conquests, the booty – all these lay open to me. Victory, and eternal fame, awaited me, curled up in the womb of history. At the foot of the mountains we could rest, even though we knew that Scipio waited there with the Roman legions – Scipio, whose cavalry had clashed with ours in the very first days of the Carthaginian entry into France, who had at once guessed at my mad, impossible intention, and pulled back into Italy to await me if the madness were after all to be sanity, and the impossible intention to become the incredible reality. Nearly twenty years later, another Scipio, son of the one who now waited for me far below, would do what no man until then could do though many were to try; he would face me in a pitched battle with an entire army on each side committed to it, and defeat me utterly. But for the moment, victory lay before me, and all I had to do was to rally my men for the final endeavour:

> 'You are now crossing the fence that encloses Italy – you can say that you are over the walls of Rome herself. From now on, there is no more climbing, and our journey lies downhill all the way. Soon, when you have fought another few battles, you will have the capital of Italy, the heart of Rome, in your hands.'

And they very nearly did. When the Carthaginian army had struggled down to the plain, his first thought, as always, was for the well-being of his men, knowing that they would soon have to fight fresh and well-fed Roman soldiers. They were in no condition to do so, as Polybius testified:

> The entire army had suffered frightfully from the effort of the climb and descent and the narrow, broken paths; they had also undergone terrible privations from the lack of food and even the simplest bodily necessities. The combination of unceasing physical effort and want of victuals had produced in many a state of utter hopelessness, and the survivors, from the effects of the appalling hardships they had had to endure, had finished the journey looking and feeling more like savage animals than men.

Animals or men, they caused consternation in Rome; the last certain news the capital had had of Hannibal, five months earlier, was of his success in the battle of Saguntum, the point from which his epic march had started. Now, he was over the Alps and safely down on the Italian plain. Fortunately for Rome's peace of mind, no one there could foresee the future, the years that lay ahead as Hannibal roamed Italy, annihilating one Roman army after another. He had never forgotten the oath he swore as a nine-year-old – always to be an enemy to Rome. What the child had promised then, the man was now to perform.

Hannibal lived for another thirty-five years. For the first sixteen of them he fought Rome, winning pitched battles against everything and everyone Rome could find to face him. He began to fail only when Fabius Cunctator devised a strategy of never facing him on the field, wearing him down instead with a policy of 'scorched earth' and relentless harassment. (Hannibal was an early master of psychological warfare; he gave orders that the countryside round Fabius' private estate should be ravaged, but the Cunctator's property left severely alone, in order to promote among the Romans suspicions of treachery on his part.)

First, though, Hannibal's military genius asserted itself in a series of encounters the like of which the world had never seen. At the Ticinus, the Trebbia, Lake Trasimene, he cut down the flower of Rome's hitherto invincible legions; Roman general after Roman general fell on those bloody fields, alongside thousands upon thousands of their troops. And then, at the Battle of Cannae, Hannibal achieved the most stupendous victory in all history; no single army, in no single day's battle – not even the battles of the Second or even the First World War – has ever lost as many men as the Romans did at Cannae.

In the end, the Fabian tactics won. Rome was ultimately inexhaustible, while Hannibal had to live off the land and scratch around for new troops (the elephants had long since died, of cold rather than wounds); when Carthage finally sent reinforcements under his brother Hasdrubal, they were trapped and slaughtered, and Hasdrubal's head was flung into Hannibal's camp. 'Now at last', he said when it was brought to him, 'I see the destiny of Carthage plain.'

He was recalled to Carthage in 202, where he was finally routed by Scipio Africanus at the Battle of Zama. The rest of his life was spent in exile, with a Roman price on his head. He could never stay long in one place; the rulers who gave him refuge knew that in doing so they were incurring the enmity of Rome. But while he was living at Ephesus, his conqueror, Scipio, visited the city, without an army, and the two mighty adversaries met.

The meeting was friendly – it is always the civilians who keep hate alive after a war – and the two talked, inevitably, of battles long ago. Scipio asked Hannibal whom he considered the world's greatest general. 'Alexander the Great', said Hannibal. 'And next after him?' asked Scipio. 'Pyrrhus', Hannibal replied. 'And third?' 'Myself'. Scipio laughed. Then he asked: 'What would you have said if you had beaten me?' 'Why then', said Hannibal, 'I would have thought myself the greatest of them all.'

He ended his life at Bythinia, another of the little kingdoms that had sheltered him. Rome had demanded that he be given up, and Roman soldiers were in the city to take him. He eluded them by taking poison –

it was said he kept it in a ring; he was sixty-four years old, and was no more afraid of death then than he had been on the battlefield long ago. His last words were characteristic of him; 'Let us now put an end to the great anxiety of the Romans, who have thought it too lengthy and too onerous a task to wait for the death of an old man whom they hate.'

And so he disappears into history, his fame wrapped about him like the cloak in which, years before, he had slept on the bare ground among his soldiers. But there is another remark of his that deserves to be remembered. In one of the cities of his long exile, he went to a lecture, by a Professor called Phormio, on military strategy – a subject, after all, of which Hannibal might be presumed to have some knowledge. Someone asked him, after the lecture, what he had thought of it. The soldier's answer was soldierly, and direct: 'I have met some old fools in my time,' he said, 'but this one beats the lot.' It had more than once occurred to me, on my own Hannibalic expedition, that his words would make a perfect epitaph for my own tombstone.

A hundred yards across the border, I was overcome with a wild desire to make snowballs and pelt a stout, pompous-looking gentleman in mutton-chop whiskers and a top hat; unfortunately, no such figure loomed out of the snow, nor indeed did any figure. I was alone on the mountain, but the urge would not leave me, and presently I knelt down in the snow, gathered a heap of it towards me, and fashioned snowballs, which I then proceeded to fling into the valley, where they vanished silently into the now blinding air.

I marched on down towards my coffee, happy, light-headed and even warm. Presently, I began to sing, at first quietly, to myself, and then, when I realised how absurd it was to be afraid of waking the neighbours, more and more loudly, though however loud my singing, the snow swallowed it, and no answering echo came back. It was some minutes more before I realised what it was that I was singing to the ungrateful hills. A less appropriate anthem could hardly be imagined; it was *Siegfried's Journey to the Rhine*. I stopped singing and began to laugh.

46 Why does St Véran need a taxidermist?   47-8 The rain turns to snow . . . and starts to settle

Acknowledgment Extraordinary, or: six weeks with six friends

I HAVE NEVER believed that a theatre audience wants to know what goes on behind the scenes, let alone how the illusion for which disbelief is so willingly suspended has been created. A playgoer who scans the stage in Act III, Scene iv of *Macbeth* in search of Banquo slipping into his place is rare – and, more to the point, foolish, for however well we know the play we must, if the scene is to achieve the effect which Shakespeare intended, deceive ourselves into believing that we do not know that a ghost is about to materialise before us; we must share Macbeth's terror ('Which of you have done this?') at the sight of the bloodstained spectre.

This voluntary stifling of our knowledge is one of the most remarkable aspects of all the performing arts; we know that the body in the library will get up and walk away as soon as the scene ends, that the Lear we have just seen die is going to take off his beard in his dressing-room and go off blithely to supper, yet we leave our hold on reality in the cloakroom, along with our coats, for the duration of the performance, without even thinking how strange a thing it is that we are doing – believing and not believing, knowing and not knowing, rejecting and accepting.

It is even more strange in the cinema, where we even manage to forget that these images are two-dimensional, and it is stranger still with television, where a palace can be two feet high and sitting on the hearthrug without exciting our astonishment, let alone scepticism.

The illusion is all; but the point is that it would be nothing if we refused to co-operate. I believe that audiences understand this point, and that that is why they reject offers to explain how the trick is done, and decline invitations to station themselves in the wings or behind the cameras.

On the other hand, they are not mad. If they see a scene on television in which a man is talking directly to them they know that he must have been talking to a camera, and that someone must therefore have been operating that camera; a moment's further thought will reveal that there must have been a director, a sound recordist and (in, say, a costume drama) anything up to a score more men and women whose contributions are essential if the viewer is to see the finished picture.

These irreconcilable views posed a problem for me. The journey of which this book tells was filmed for television as it was taking place, by a team of six, in whose company I therefore spent many hours filming, eating and relaxing. In any such project (it took six weeks) there will be episodes off-screen, from misunderstandings to technical hitches, and from dangers skirted to laughter shared. None of this appears in my book; just as the viewers of the television series will not see the camera, the microphone or those involved in operating them, even though the viewers know perfectly well that the machinery and those in charge of it must have existed, so the readers will not hear of what befell machines or machinists, even though they know that other people were present.

That, as I say, is what I believe audiences want. Nevertheless, I would be the basest ingrate if, in thus abiding by the convention, I were to ignore my colleagues' existence altogether. But a mere note of thanks will not suffice to repay either the pleasure and stimulus of their company or the no less great helpfulness and solicitude they displayed, let alone both. I therefore intend to call the roll of an *équipe* who, beginning as strangers to me, rapidly became the firmest of friends.

The director was Bernard Clark, a man of the most astonishing resourcefulness; he drove over the whole route in advance of the filming and, despite the fact that he speaks not a word of French, managed to line up an enormous proportion of the contracts, permissions, interviewees, logistical supports and material resources that would be required along the line of march. When I say that he spoke no French at all I mean it, but it never seemed to inhibit him, let alone defeat him; when pursuing me while I was off walking unfilmed he would hail people working in the fields and ask them such questions as 'Mon friend perambulateur that way?' or 'Monsieur dans the hat, oui?', and such was the fervour of his demeanour that he invariably got a reply in the form of a pointing finger. But the care he took of me, which ranged from finding me English newspapers in the most improbably remote places to invariably helping me off with my rucksack, leaves me permanently in his debt, while the unflagging enthusiasm he generated from beginning to end inspired us all.

The chief cameraman, Graham Eggar, is without exception the hardest worker I have ever known in any field. If a shot of me walking over a bridge would be more effective filmed from the river beneath it, he would unhesitatingly suggest shooting it while standing up to his knees in icy water, and promptly suit his action to his suggestion. After the close of a film-session that left us all exhausted he would invariably think of a few more shots that might add something further to the finished film, and set up the camera to take them.

The assistant cameraman, David Eggar (Graham's son), a gentle blond giant with a dry wit that took the form of immense mock-complaints at the hardships he was forced to endure, had little reason to feel affectionate towards me – indeed, had I known the truth I would have gone in fear of my life from him, but he manfully concealed from me until the last night but one of the filming that he had been called away to take part when he was *three days into his honeymoon.* Yet so far from resenting me, he went far out of his way to help me at every turn.

Steven Egleton, the sound-recordist, a largely silent Tynesider who did not conceal his contempt for a country that could not supply him with his regular intake of Newcastle Brown, was a rock of calm even when tempers were beginning to fray and exhaustion was setting in; I shall remember him particularly on the climb to the Col des Aiguilles, a tiny, yellow-clad dot far above me, moving up at an absolutely unvaried pace which typified his whole approach to his work and, I guess, to life itself.

Michael Hutchinson, the assistant producer, who spoke fluent French, was the only member of the party to sustain real injury; after a tangle with a recalcitrant donkey he finished the trip on crutches. But his cheerfulness and wit were the same after the accident as before it; and I owe him particular thanks for repeatedly booking my hotel rooms in the villages that I estimated I would reach by nightfall on each day of the next section of the march.

The only woman in the party was Nathalie Ferrier, the production assistant; half-Swiss, she was virtually bilingual, but her role as interpreter was only one of the long list of labours that she shouldered, and the charm that she brought to what would otherwise inevitably have been an almost unbearably introspective male group softened and enhanced the atmosphere throughout; she, too, was exceptionally assiduous in seeing that I wanted for nothing to make my own contribution easier.

There were, of course, many other people involved in putting the journey on to the television screen. But these six people were my companions throughout, and even when I was off on my own the pleasure of working with them, and the friendship they extended to me so generously, made the kilometres fly unnoticed beneath my boots. I thank and salute them all.

Index

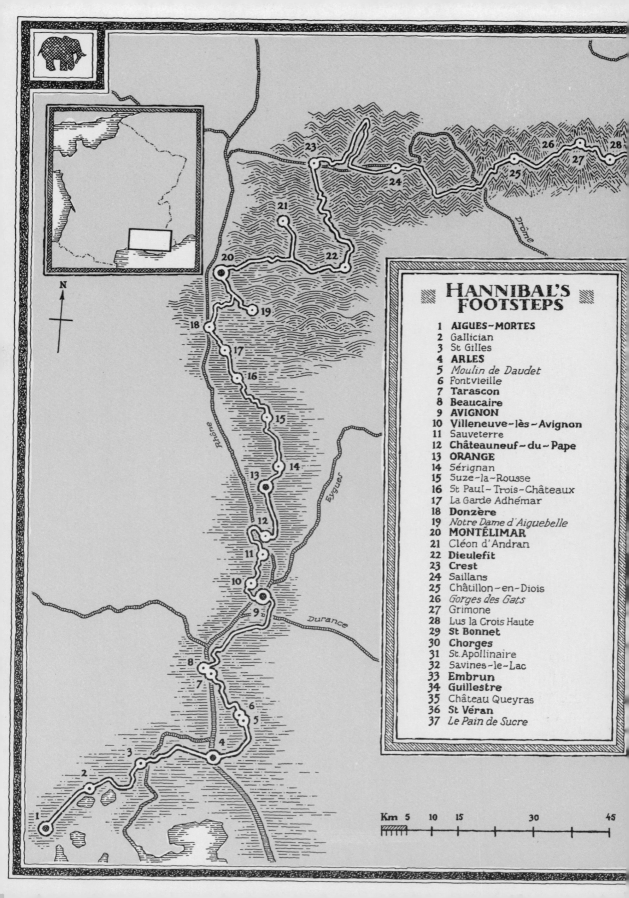

HANNIBAL'S FOOTSTEPS

1 **AIGUES~MORTES**
2 Gallician
3 St Gilles
4 **ARLES**
5 *Moulin de Daudet*
6 Fontvieille
7 **Tarascon**
8 **Beaucaire**
9 **AVIGNON**
10 **Villeneuve~lès~Avignon**
11 Sauveterre
12 **Châteauneuf~du~Pape**
13 **ORANGE**
14 Sérignan
15 Suze~la~Rousse
16 St Paul~Trois~Châteaux
17 La Garde Adhémar
18 **Donzère**
19 *Notre Dame d'Aiguebelle*
20 **MONTÉLIMAR**
21 Cléon d'Andran
22 **Dieulefit**
23 **Crest**
24 Saillans
25 Châtillon~en~Diois
26 *Gorges des Gats*
27 Grimone
28 Lus la Crois Haute
29 **St Bonnet**
30 **Chorges**
31 St.Apollinaire
32 Savines~le~Lac
33 **Embrun**
34 **Guillestre**
35 Château Queyras
36 **St Véran**
37 *Le Pain de Sucre*

N

Km 5   10   15   30   45